Confessions
of a Sex Addict

by

Kelly D. Boykin

Dedication

This book has been a labor of love, and without the support of my family and friends, it may never have seen the light of day. So, to my mom, Shirley; my daughters, Kayla and Shannon; my friends, Carla, Kay, Shannon, Lacey, Teddy, Cliff, Chrissy, and the rest; and to my brothers and sisters, I say 'thank you' for standing by me; it's amazing how much of my craziness you have all endured while finding a way to love me anyway.

If you're in crisis, please contact:

THE NATIONAL SUICIDE PREVENTION LIFELINE

If you're feeling desperate, alone or hopeless, call the National Suicide Prevention Lifeline at: (800) 273-TALK (8255). It's a free, 24-hour hotline available to anyone in suicidal crisis or emotional distress. Your call will be routed to the crisis center nearest to you.

Contents

Preface: Stealing Souls

When I entered the tiny subdivision, I was immediately taken by the pride of the homeowners and their sense of community. Flower beds abounded with the reds, oranges, and purples of springtime in the desert. Manicured lawns with kids' bikes and twirling sprinklers welcomed me.

It didn't matter that the spaces were occupied by white homes on wheels, axels hidden by white skirting, concrete porches covered by ornamental tin, and shutters painted in varying shades of blue.

What mattered, really, was the hope these homes revealed; hope for a better life. You could almost feel the collective breath held; the desperation to never go back to places occupied before. I so desperately wanted to hold onto that hope for myself. I wanted to feel the calm. I wanted to see what they saw, but looks can be deceiving.

What I saw in that peaceful place was the horror and pain being inflicted upon the innocent inside the home that occupies space #207. Inside that home was a young girl, long black hair draped across a pillow covered in sweat, her wrists tied to the bedposts, lit cigarettes laid upon her naked brown flesh, her mouth open in a scream with no sound.

In the corner sat a man full of malice, glowing in evil pride at his handiwork. The wooden chair in which he sat creaked as he leaned forward in anticipation of his guests' arrival.

In his minds-eye he could see the looks on the faces of the young boys he called sons; he could almost feel their shock and horror at the sight before them. He could almost feel the disgust their teenaged erections would bring. He knew that forcing them to take his prize would be a risk. What he also knew was that their fear of him was already so strong, brought on by years of physical and emotional abuse, that his sons could not object. The thought only proved to heighten his own arousal and give him that ever-growing control he craved.

When the man heard the knock on the door, he looked at the girl and stroked his erection. He stood and made his way to the front door. As he passed the entry to the kitchen he saw his wife, handcuffed to the refrigerator, beaten and slumped on the floor where he'd left her. A brief, but satisfied, smile crossed his face.

Grabbing three beers from the ice chest next to the front door, the man turned the knob and let his sons enter. He handed each the cold elixir and said, "Come on, I have a surprise for you." The quizzical look and fear were more than the man had even hoped as each boy entered the room and saw the girl tied to the bed.

The man who called himself dad said, "Go ahead. Take a turn. She wants you to." Each turned and looked at the other; they didn't know what to do or how to react to the scene before them. So they stood and waited.

Growing impatient, the man raised his voice and said, "Boys! Dad got you a nice present and you're going to enjoy it!" As each boy unwrapped their gift, their manhood the scissors that cut her ribbon, the man sat in his creaky wooden chair and unwrapped himself to her screams.

The boys left as quickly as they came, leaving their childhood behind in a puddle of semen on her thighs.

Introduction

At the tender age of three, my biological father started molesting me; using me for his pleasure, really. The abuse went on for years and finally ended when I found my voice at the age of 15. I've dealt with the pain of it for most of my life. Between the flashbacks, hating myself, self-abuse, feeling worthless and alone, and a twelve-year struggle with sexual addiction, it's been a battle to stay whole and alive. I've tried very hard to not let the abuse be the "thing" that defines me, but it has been a difficult struggle.

For years and years, I held onto this "secret" part of me; that part of me that wanted to be loved and held and safe, but instead manifested itself into a sexual addiction and a bevy of lies. Even though I had told people about the abuse, it was easier to keep secret the shame I felt, while continuing to lie to myself and others about what those secrets were doing to me.

The biggest hurdle was getting over the victim mentality I carried around with me. Being a victim was a necessary aspect of my recovery, both from the abuse and the sexual addiction, but it wasn't a state I needed to be in forever. I had to find a way to get past that way of thinking and into the mode of survivor. I had to allow myself to remember what he did, even if I was afraid, so I could deal with the pain and come out whole on the other side.

Part of my journey to healing was through journaling. I found a great site online and let it all pour out. Because I had already labeled myself a sex addict, I initially wrote about the sex act, itself. I guess I thought it was "cool" to write about all the sex I was having. It only took a week to realize how ridiculous that really was. I read the words I had written and felt kind of nauseous; I was sad about how I portrayed myself. See, regardless of my behavior, I knew deep down that I was a good, kind, compassionate, and loving person, and not only a sex addict. I realized that to glorify the disease would be to simply feed into all the misconceptions already out there. I realized I was a sex addict *because* of the abuse, and not because I was an immoral slut, and it was then I started telling my story.

My real story is about a girl who endured years of sexual abuse at the hands of her biological father and the adult who survived to tell about it. It was difficult in the beginning, but I just let myself write. I knew I was completely anonymous and could say whatever I wanted, so I did. It was pretty liberating.

I wrote about sex, childhood abuse, relationships, fear, my own paranoia, having hope, and overcoming obstacles. For me, it was as if I were finally free to just be myself, even though no one knew who I was.

The anonymity an online journal afforded me made a huge difference in what I wrote about and the words I chose. I wasn't afraid that bio-dad would find the pages and kill me like he threatened all those years. I wasn't afraid to be that scared little girl I regularly hid from my boyfriend. I wasn't afraid to show my vulnerabilities because I knew no one could use them against me. I was anonymous, and free to say whatever I felt. All the rage, anger, pain, sadness, depression, and bad choices I've made came out and helped rid me of some of the shit I was holding onto.

After two years of journaling, I felt like a new person. I knew that the sex addict was gone and a new 'me' had emerged. I am still on a path of discovery, but know the former me no longer has the control she once did.

The next phase of my journey is telling my story to you. I've contemplated this book again and again, and wondered how much of myself I should reveal. Because I now know how important it is to be completely honest, I've decided to include many of the journal entries I wrote during that two year period. Yes, it's hard to imagine the number of people who will read this book, my name included, and KNOW what I did and who I was then, but it's important. If I want to help affect change, I have to be willing to lay out my soul for your review; I have to be honest in order to squash the secrets and the shame. My hope is that you get a good understanding of where my head was and how I got through it to the place I am now.

I guess what I want most is for you to learn from my experiences and understand that you're not alone. Yes, we do some stupid things and put ourselves in risky situations, but those things are not a true reflection of who we are inside. Who we are on the inside is magnificent, and worthy, and loving, and unique. Embrace it and let the journey begin.

(Throughout the book you'll find chapters relating to different subject matter, such as addictions, relationships, counseling, etc. Each chapter has an introduction then several journal entries, which are indicated with a title in bold, along with the date the entry was originally written.)

Chapter One: Screaming from the Rooftop

My real-life friends knew almost nothing about my life as a sex addict. There were six of us (all women) who got together on Friday nights to drink, talk, and play cards. Common sense would have you believe they all knew what I was doing, but they didn't. I had a knack for appearing to be an open book, even though I kept a big part of my life secret. To my friends, I was intelligent, funny, a successful business owner, a good mom, and much too busy to have a steady man in my life. They had no idea I had several men in my life, all of whom helped fulfill a need I couldn't then identify.

When I started my journal, I remember sitting at my desk and being elated that I had found an outlet for talking about the secret life I had been leading. Even though, outwardly, I pretended there was nothing wrong with what I was doing, I knew there was. Why would I keep so many secrets otherwise?

I was worried about what to write in that first entry, but my sexual addiction was eating me up and I needed a place to purge.

I needed someone to know about what I was doing, and it seemed an anonymous group of friends was the next best option, so I sat and wrote…

Stranger than fiction:

Tue, 27 Jul 2004

I am a sex addict. I have to admit that now. It has taken many years to finally say it and believe it but now I'm ready to deal and move on.

This journal will be a reflection of my soul and a story of my day.

Welcome.

Day One

Tue, 27 Jul 2004

I'm sitting here patiently waiting for the phone to ring. One of my guys, MG, is supposed to call so we can hook up. I'm totally becoming addicted to having sex with him. First of all, his dick is beautiful. It's nice sized, a little on the large size (yippee), and the head is perfect.

Secondly, when we have sex it's like two wild animals being unleashed on each other. I always start by giving him head, which I have perfected over the years. He loves it, I love it, and I take my time. It's like magic in my mouth. The feeling of his dick in my mouth is one of the best sensations in the world to me. I think that's why he enjoys it so much; he knows that I do too.

We then move on to actual sex. We try different positions to prolong the pleasure but we always end up doggy style. And wow is all I can say. He fucks me so hard, spanks my ass, grabs a handful of hair and gently pulls. I can barely contain myself. I scream his name and damn! Whew! I'm getting all wet thinking about having him.

The bad part is that I love sex with him so much that sex with anyone else just isn't as satisfying to me anymore. Well, I do have a great time with MP. I think he would be a complete freak if we were in the right situation, but that hasn't presented itself yet. Maybe soon, though.

Well, MG just called and I'm on my way; short skirt, no panties, a good time in the making. I'll check back tomorrow.

Just when you think....

Wed, 28 Jul 2004

My time with MG was great last night. The oral was great, as usual, and I really took my time. I think the only appropriate word to describe the way his dick feels in my mouth is extraordinary. Wonderful. Delicious. Mmmmmm. Wow. I know that's several words, but man, it was so nice.

He pulled out some extra moves too! It was so erotic I thought I was going to come out of my skin. He knows how to touch me in just the right spot, in the just the right way, circling, stroking, slow, fast, teasing, licking, pinching, and spanking (which is one of my favorite things).

I made sure to suck him off one more time before I left so he would go to sleep thinking of the pleasure and of me.

So here's the problem, I want more. And the more I get, the more I want. It's like this weird cyclical thing. You'd think I would be satisfied after a night like that, but I'm not. I just want more and more and more. I'm ready to call one of my other guys to get some tonight. I've already seen three of them this week so I'll have to pick guy #4 and hope he's available.

Here's another problem, I have a boyfriend. He lives in a different area so I don't get to see him very often, but I do love him. I know, how the hell can I say that when I'm fucking four other guys? Well, the other guys are just about sex and that's all. He doesn't know and I won't tell him. I'm not even sure where our relationship stands at this point, but that's another story.

Anyway, I better run for now.

Let's get serious!

Wed, 28 Jul 2004

This whole journal writing experience is causing me a little pain and self-reflection. I know I have to be honest about my experiences but not in a way that will try to glamorize the illness that truly lies behind it.

I haven't decided whether I love sex or if I just don't know what else to do with my pain. I think the latter is probably the most appropriate, although I want to believe the former.

Some people don't understand the disease. They think sex addicts are just a bunch of slutty nymphs with no morals. Most sex addicts are people who have been used and abused, in some sort, as children. For me, I was molested for years by my father. Then raped at 18. Then sexually abused for years by my husband. Yeah, we were married, but that doesn't give him the right to degrade and humiliate me for his gratification. I never learned what real love is. "Love" has always been sexualized by the people who used me and when you're three years old, you don't know any better.

I don't know what to do at this point or how to handle the situation. I know that I like the feeling sex gives me. It acts as a stress reliever and makes me feel wanted. I hate not feeling wanted. I hate not feeling like I'm worthy of love. I hate that no one wants me. I hate that these fucking men decided it was okay to take my childhood (and my trust) in their hands and squeeze the life out of it. No, I don't hate all men, I only feel pity for the men who abused me; just think of the hate they must have for themselves.

Stranger than fiction:

Thu, 29 Jul 2004

Sweet

Hard

Delicious

Everything I want in a dick

Sweet

Hard

Delicious

Everything I want in my pussy

Masturbation and Donuts

Fri, 30 Jul 2004

I'm trying so hard to not masturbate today. I love the warm, wet feeling of my pussy but I know that I need to take a break. It's like eating donuts; they are really great at first, but then the sugar turns to fat which then makes your ass the size of Texas which then causes you to have fewer dates which then depresses you so you eat more donuts and the cycle continues. Masturbation is just like that. It starts out innocently enough, you're stressed out and need a relief, then you start doing it every morning, then at work during lunch cause the thrill of someone catching you is so cool, then on the way home while driving your car, then suddenly you can't function because your hand is always playing with your pussy, then you become immune to dick. Oh it's a vicious cycle.

So, I haven't done it today and will try to refrain. Maybe I'll go get a donut!

Fuck You
Sat, 31 Jul 2004
I'm a fucking girl and sometimes I just need to hear that you love me and miss me and think I'm the fucking shit! I'm tired of being strong all the damned time. Sometimes I'm just scared and want you to hold me. Man you piss me off sometimes. Fuck you! Right in the neck!

Gimme some chocolate
Sat, 31 Jul 2004
So it's finally happened... I have absolutely no urge to have sex today! Too much on my mind, I guess. I've been trying to decide whether or not to post my story, my motivation and my thoughts on why I am who I am. I'm not sure what's holding me up. Part of me wants to say everything and part of me wants to continue to hide. Maybe I'm afraid that if I say it then it becomes real and I'll have to actually deal with it.

In some ways, I like who I am right now, sexual addiction and all. I like having sex, talking about sex, watching sex, smelling sex, etc. Is this healthy and normal or am I just a freak? I know I use sex to relieve my stress. I also know that I use it to feel wanted by another human being. I walk around all confident but I'm so scared that I'm going to die alone because no one will want me. I hate that feeling most of all and it's a hard one to change.

It's weird to talk to my friends because they say that I'm strong and confident and that I can do anything. I can't see that in myself. I think I just ACT strong and confident to fool everyone including myself. Lying to yourself is a bad habit to get into. Pretty soon you don't even know who you really are. I feel so fucking insane sometimes, oh wait, but I appear perfectly normal to the outside world. Gr.

Well, I guess I'll just continue to think about it and see what happens.

Chapter Two:
The real story

Courage is the first of human qualities because it is the quality which guarantees the others.

~ Aristotle

My first week of journaling was pretty intense, mainly because I knew I was better than the woman I portrayed myself to be, but also because it brought up memories I had been stuffing away for too long. After that first week, I took my first real glimpse in the mirror and started to write the real story...

The beginning

Tue, 03 Aug 2004

It all started when I was three years old. Apparently, my biological father thought it was a great idea to have sex with me, because we all know how fucking sexy three year olds are! Anyway, my first memory is made up of bits and pieces but I mostly remember his hands. He had hair on his knuckles and his fingernails were dirty. I was lying in a bed underneath the most beautiful patchwork quilt. The squares were velvety and soft and my hair was laid out on the pillow. The bed itself was wooden and four-poster. It was sitting on top of a round platform stage. The carpet was a light, almost slate blue. I can still see how the fibers were woven together and twisted around to make the carpet whole. There were two other people in the room; a woman who was smiling at me and a man behind an old 8mm-type camera.

Everything seemed loving and fine until bio-dad's hand came towards me and he keep repeating over and over that he loved me. The action itself wasn't scary but the intent was; you can sense when something is wrong, even that young.

The woman kept smiling at me and she was holding her hands together in front of her in a strange way. It was almost as if she were one of those etiquette teachers who taught you how to stand like a proper lady. After awhile, when she sensed that I was scared, her face turned red and mean. She was yelling something that I don't remember.

In retrospect, the man behind the camera seemed very much like a follower; like someone who can't make his own decisions. He kept peeking out from behind the camera to more closely watch what was happening.

A strange phenomenon happens when you're being abused in such a manner, your mind sometimes removes you from the scene because it is too much to bear. It's called disassociation. For me, it was as if I were watching a movie... from my spot on the ceiling.

I was sort of floating on the ceiling watching this cute little girl get used and abused and tortured by her father and his minions. It was as if I were not the one actually being molested. It was that other little girl down there on the bed. That other little girl was studying carpet fibers in order to detach. That other little girl thought her daddy loved her. That other little girl was screaming. From my spot on the ceiling, that other little girl wasn't me.

Over the years and as an adult, I still do that detaching thing. It's caused me to lose a substantial amount of memory. My childhood was snatched from me at three years old and continued to be taken away year after year.

Struggling with honesty
Wed, 04 Aug 2004

I'm having a hard day today. I believe it's because I started to tell my story and now I'm reliving some of it. Not so much with flashbacks or anything like that, just that I am now thinking about it more and it's making me angry. Yes, I have forgiven bio-dad for his actions but I guess I am still holding on to some shit.

I disassociated a lot during that time and even now as an adult. While the abuse was happening, I would concentrate on one object in the room as a means of distracting myself from what was happening. Sometimes I would study the carpet, sometimes I would think about flying above the trees, sometimes I just wanted to die.

I remember smells, textures, facial features. If I smell certain things, even today, it will cause me to either cringe or go into a small anxiety attack. I can't eat certain foods because of the texture. And if I see a man with a mustache and crooked little mouth, I just want to fucking clock him.

I can still see that fucking smile on bio-dads face! It seriously makes me want to vomit. I guess that's why I have such an easy time leaving my body. I don't want to remember. That has become a problem in my adult life; I have such a huge memory loss now. I have a hard time remembering small events that happened six months ago because my mind is so used to storing memory in a really fucked up way. I remember vaguely being somewhere, but not conversations, who I was with, etc. But I do remember feelings. It's weird.

I continued to have nightmares until I was 33 years old. I would dream that I was standing outside and he was telling me that I would have to die for telling his (our) secret. His voice was soft and menacing. The guy behind the camera would suddenly appear and would be holding a gun. He would shoot me while bio-dad just stood behind him. I could see the bullet holes in my body but there was no blood (a few times I saw blood but I don't know what that means).

I was scared of bio-dad because he threatened me and totally fucked with my brain! I know that he was in prison for armed robbery when I was very young. He killed someone when I was 14 or so. He wasn't convicted because the cops called it "justifiable." Fuck that! He beat the dude to death with a fucking lead pipe. It's just that the other guy was a criminal too and the cops were happy to be rid of him. He used to torture his wives by tying them up and placing several lit cigarettes on various places on their body, then watch while his friend (or an unwilling family member) fucked her. She's screaming and being raped and he watches. It's no wonder I took his threats seriously.

I could go on and on but I have to stop for now. It's funny stuff man. If I wasn't part of the shit, I wouldn't fucking believe that any man could be so fucking evil and still be alive and not in jail. My only solace is that I know he has a front row seat at the gates of hell. Not only is his life a living-hell but he'll have to spend eternity there, as well.

Abuse, Addiction and Normality

Sat, 07 Aug 2004

Strange things happen when you've been sexualized from the age of three. I was too young to understand what was happening to me but I knew it was wrong. I remember wanting to pull off my skin and not knowing why. I've felt completely insane most of my life.

When you're so young and your father molests you while telling you that he loves you while torturing you while letting other people rape and torture you while threatening you and making you feel like the whole world is in on the sick joke, your view of normal sexuality gets a little fucked up. No, it gets a lot fucked up.

I went through a period of promiscuity when I was about 18 years old or so. I felt completely numb during sex. It's not that I didn't want to have sex but it's not that I really wanted to either. I was just there and the guy could do to me whatever he wanted; I didn't feel as if I could say no. My body had been used so much before that I thought that's the way it was supposed to be. It almost makes me sick to think about some of things that I allowed people to do to me. (As I am writing this, I just realized that even though I've lost most of my memory, I do remember the name of every person I've ever slept with; how weird is that?)

Also, when I was 18, I was raped by my boyfriend's roommate. I woke up to find him straddling me and pulling my legs apart. I was startled and sickened that this could be happening again, but I didn't feel as if I could say no. I just lay there lifeless and crying. In my minds' eye right now, I can see his fucking face hovering over me and twisting in ecstasy at my expense.

I never told anyone until ten years later when I called the police and gave them a description of him (once a rapist, always a rapist) and then I called his house. His wife answered and said he wasn't home. She asked if she could take a message so I said, "Well, your husband raped me ten years ago and I just wanted you to know that I've called the police." Of course he was there and of course he picked up the phone. I repeated the message to him and told him that if he's raped since me or plans on raping again, the police have a good description of him including his phone number and address. Whew! That felt so fucking good to do. I know the police couldn't do anything but it felt good nonetheless.

I have gone through the promiscuous thing a few more times since then but I'm working on being normal, whatever the hell that is. I know that I'm a sex addict now and I'm working on trying to figure out what triggers I need to pay attention to. I haven't had sex in over a week now so I think I'm doing pretty well. I've gone from not knowing how to say "no" to saying "yes" all the damned time. It's my way of controlling my sexuality so I'm not taken advantage of again. What a warped since of reality I'm living in, but it is my reality and actually "normal" for many survivors of childhood sexual abuse.

A Mother`s Guilt

Mon, 09 Aug 2004

I've been sitting her for over half an hour trying to write something about my mom. I've written, rewritten, then finally erased the whole mess and am starting over with this entry.

The problem is that I'm not sure exactly how I feel about her right now. My mom is a wonderful person with great intentions and a few quirks. She's had a very rough life and has come through it pretty well. I guess I'm just slightly pissed at her and I'm not sure what to do with the feeling.

The reason I'm pissed is because we've never been able to have any kind of meaningful conversation about what bio-dad did to me. I told her about the abuse when I was 28 years old and her first response was, "are you sure?" Hell yeah I'm fucking sure! She feels guilty because "she should have known" (her words not mine) and should have been able to stop it. I've told her many, many times that I do not blame her for any of it; he made those choices and was clever enough to keep it away from her. I truly do not blame her but she is so guilt-ridden that we can't even talk about it.

I need to be able to talk to her about some things, to help fill in some holes from my childhood, etc., but she just can't handle it. I know that I may never get the answers but dammit, she's my mom and I need her. I think it's her responsibility to step outside of her own guilt and talk. Maybe I'm wrong about that but I don't have anyone else to ask those questions of. She holds the key to my memory box and she won't give it up.

I haven't told my mom that I'm mad at her and I'm not sure I will. Because of her guilt and constant worry, I may just reconcile that I'll never have the answers and let her start her retirement without worrying about me. Hell, I don't know. It's just so fucking frustrating.

This is love?

Mon, 16 Aug 2004

I wish you could feel their love
I wish you could see their pain
For their souls are eating them alive
Guilty pleasure, depravity, longing
Wishing they could stop
Without understanding they can
Filled with self-loathing and shame
While denying anything is wrong
Continuing to rob the child
Taking what can never be returned

I want to remember being a child, let me rephrase, a HAPPY child. I hear stories about myself as if I were a visitor in my own life but I have no sight, sound or smell to help me recover them on my own. I might as well be listening to stories about the neighbor two doors down; it would all sound the same to me, anyway.

The reality of the situation is that the bad memories have robbed me of the happy memories I'm sure are there. It's a means of survival, I know. It's just so strange to sit in a room with my family, hearing their funny stories and laughter, pretending I remember the fish Uncle Larry caught, all-the-while feeling as if I'm an intruder listening to personal family things. I'm an observer; an easy chair in the corner, melding into the background with plaids of brown and blue. I want to run and return to the safety of my own mind but I sit and listen with a forced smile and nod.

It's not just that I miss my memories, but I miss my family. If only there were a magic eraser that could selectively take the bad and replace it with the good so that feeling of being all alone in a room full of people would stop.

May God have mercy on the souls of those who steal the innocence and memories from a child.

Blue broken dream
Wed, 15 Dec 2004
I'm the last one left
there's nowhere to go
but farther into myself

hiding behind this mask
has not served me well
but it's all I know
and all I trust

the sky is grey
the mood is dark
my face void of all emotion
except the lines of worry and a frown

your eyes don't see
what I want them to see

only that which I portray
in my little picture world
drawn with broken crayons
on paper bags

standing before the pile
I light the match
and set aflame all my hopes and dreams
should I shed a tear for things not found
but lost in the chaos?
what's the point?
Is there really a meaning of life?

The death of innocence
Tue, 21 Dec 2004

I've been thinking a lot about what I would do if I found out my bio-dad died?

Would I dance around? Would I feel sad? Would I feel like that chapter of my life was finally done? I truly don't know. I'd like to believe that it would affect me, but it's been so long since I removed myself from him and his depravity, I don't know if I can feel anything for him at all. In life, he's nothing to me but a bad memory; someone who decided to fuck up my life without any thought. Bio-dad scarred me in so many ways. I've forgiven his deeds but I have not forgotten - that almost seems impossible to do. But how would I feel if he died? "Nothing" is what comes to mind.

I'm a kind person. How can I possibly think to feel *nothing* for the man who helped give me life? It begs the question, "how could he molest the child he helped give life to?" It's a tough question with no answer - none I'll ever receive anyway.

I guess I just feel numb. It's not only this contemplation that makes me feel numb; it's the totality of the situation. I want to heal and move on but I feel stuck where I am, as if there's no anecdote for the poison in my soul. I'm sure it's fear of knowing, fear of change, and fear of finding myself that leaves me stranded in this spot. Finding the way out is the problem. Ironically, it's also the solution.

Flying away and escaping the madness
Sun, 13 Feb 2005

When I was little and bio-dad used me for his show-and-tell pleasure, hands all over me, dick where it shouldn't be, I would escape by mentally leaving my body. I would travel to the ceiling and watch that poor little girl getting raped. I didn't like it but I wanted to make sure someone remembered. She was so sad, crying, while daddy said "I love you." Sometimes I would hide in the corner of that ceiling because I was scared, too. I was wearing my pink dress and white bobby socks, ribbon in my hair, black patent leather shoes.

Sometimes I would fly, after daddy put my panties back on and told me not to tell. I wanted to scream but I was afraid of the bullets and the other man and the lady who smiled with monster teeth. In my mind I would fly over my pretend city of green grass and rivers with tire swings. Arms outstretched, I could feel the wind cleansing me of the bad things. The sun beckoned me to go higher where the warmth was. I smiled. Until I flew too fast. The trees jumped to grab my feet and pull me down. The city turned grey and black. Arms flapping wildly to stop. I was scared. Then daddy said "I love you. I'll kill you. We are watching." I got out of my flight and the car. I rushed inside to my mom who asked, "Did you have a fun day at the zoo?" Yes. I was afraid of the bullets.

Lost souls

Wed, 02 Mar 2005 19

Looking through the glass into the room, I see myself standing there amongst the furnishings of green and taupe, cherry woods and oriental rugs. Black skirt, red blouse, and sexy new shoes. I look pretty good. I see myself talking, laughing, drinking, yet utterly alone in the crowd.

Gazing into the distance, I find you standing there, a look of bewilderment on your face. Of course, it's hidden by your dashing smile and quick wit, but I recognize it; that look is one only other pained souls can see. With a quirky little smile, I say to myself, "another thespian in act one." As you catch my stare, I really see the pain in your eyes. And you see the pain in mine. Two souls, alone in the crowd, pretending everything is okay.

Leaving your body behind, your soul joins mine on the lanai. The tropical breeze is nice. We stand together and watch ourselves alone. A warm and calming light surrounds us, protecting our spirits from our pasts. Another glance, another soul, another friend, another light. Soon we are joined by many. The souls of the other thespians in the room join our looking-glass party. Some are battered and bruised, some abused, some attacked, some still afraid, some healing. But we're amongst friends, no longer alone in the crowd, no longer alone in our pain.

Say a prayer

Sat, 19 Mar 2005
Say a prayer
for the little girls
and little boys
who, today, will have their innocence
raped
by people without souls

Say a prayer
for the little girls
and little boys
who, today, will have their bodies
beaten
by people without souls

Say a prayer
for the little girls
and little boys
who, today, will feel the pain of being
starved
by people without souls

Say a prayer
for the little girls
and little boys
who have no choice
and no defense
from these people without souls

Say a prayer
so it will stop.

The perfect prison?

Wed, 30 Mar 2005

I've often fantasized about torturing and maiming bio-dad for all the abuse he perpetrated on me for so long. Maybe duct tape him to a chair, cut his eye lids off, and make him watch as I slowly cut off other body parts - a few toes, a few fingers, a couple of stabs at his knees, cut the Achilles tendon, then the coup de' gras, his balls and dick. I would top it all off by forcefully shoving the dick and balls into his mouth so he could suffocate on them. Yes, quite a delightful fantasy.

Of course, I'd never do it. Some fantasies are meant to be played out, but this one is not. It's just a thought I sometimes have to help me get through my own pain. I'll admit that the vision of him sitting there in absolute pain brings a little smile to my face, but it's then replaced by the vision of me in prison getting fucked in the ass with a broom handle by a girl named "Molly." Not really my idea of fun, you know?

What I'd really like to see is a place, maybe a small and desolate island, where we could send and never see again, all the convicted pedophiles of this world. Each prisoner, male and female alike, would be given a 25-pound bag of rice, a jar of peanut butter, a blanket, a pillow, and a handbook called, "The Ultimate Survival Guide for Pedophiles." It would contain a first aid guide on how to repair that gaping hole in your ass after your first gang rape, information on how to properly lube up using peanut butter, and how to prepare rice for that romantic dinner with your new friend "Bubba."

The laws in this country are ridiculous in regards to prison terms for convicted pedophiles. Our lawmakers don't take into account the years of emotional pain the victim endures because of the abuse. What's sad is that most convicted pedophiles receive less jail time than someone who has stolen a car. I wonder if anyone has ever calculated how much stolen innocence is worth?

When I was seven

Sat, 07 May 2005

When you're seven years old, life should be pretty carefree. Days should be spent swimming, playing with Barbie's under the big tree out front, smiles and laughter, slip n' slides, and cartwheels with crooked legs. A child of seven should be free to wear pretty pink skirts, cowboy boots and a colander for a hat, all while believing she's the next Miss America in training. Life at seven should be devoid of pain and mistrust and fear.

When I was seven, life wasn't so magical. Although bio-dad was in and out of my life at the time, the abuse he inflicted on me escalated to a fevered-pitch. I think that's the year he started torturing me for fun and pleasure. My visual memories of that time are very dim and clouded by my minds need to survive, but the emotional memories are still very clear. What I remember most is the feeling of my head being squeezed in some sort of vice and being tied down tight. (Breathe... remember to breathe.) I remember long hair in pigtails and excruciating pain.

When I was seven, a van full of men tried to kidnap me. I can't prove it, but I believe it was on the order of bio-dad. (Maybe I was being "sold" for drugs or money.) I was walking home from the neighborhood swimming pool with my brother when a white van pulled up, the side door quickly slid open, and a man inside grabbed me. A neighbor lady sweeping her porch saw what was happening and started to scream and run towards the van swinging her broom like a ninja. I was kicking and screaming and wriggled away once. The man grabbed at me again, the lady kept running, swinging and screaming, my brother was screaming, and I got away once again. The van full of men took off. The police told my mom that I shouldn't walk around in my swimming suit.

When I was seven, I tried to kill myself for the first time. I think I was too young to truly grasp the concept of suicide, but the intent was there. I knew that the big sharp knife my mom used for cutting meat and vegetables would probably do something. I knew that you had to have a heartbeat to live and I knew where my heart was, so if I could just put the knife there the pain would stop. I took moms knife into the back yard and hid between the fence and the side of the house. I put the knife on my chest and cried. I didn't know it, but my twin brother followed me out and saw what I was doing. In our seven-year-old language, we talked. I don't remember the conversation, really, but I know that my brother saved my life that day. We took the knife back into the kitchen and never told my mom about it - we probably didn't want to get into trouble for touching the knife.

Seven was a pretty rough year. Only by the grace of God am I alive and marginally mentally-healthy today. If you know someone with a seven-year-old child, give that child a big hug for me.

Epiphany Alert!
Mon, 19 Dec 2005
Okay, so I may have figured something out... I think I may have stumbled onto the reason(s) I find it so hard to accept love.

I know what love means to me... kindness, compassion, giving of yourself unconditionally, and sticking it out through good and bad. Unfortunately, the type of love that has been shown to me is angry, hate-filled, and full of pain. I've been beaten, raped, and emotionally abused all while being told that I am loved. No wonder I'm so fucked up!

Whenever someone gets close to me and says those three little words, I get the urge to run for the hills. In my mind, the next thing I expect is a punch in the mouth or to be thrown down and kicked while being called ugly and stupid, while simultaneously being told that I am loved. My experience with "love" hasn't been that great.

I feel like I just figured out that $1 + 1 = 2$. I'm an intelligent woman. I can't believe it took me this long to finally put the pieces together. I know I've said these things before, but they were just words. Now, I actually understand the full impact of the experience.

Well. Hm. Now my goal is to figure out that $2 + 2 = 4$ and how the information will help to rewire my thoughts on love. This is a good day.

When I Was 15
Tue, 27 Dec 2005

A row of dingy trailers lined the hot and dusty street in what was the bad part of town. Drug dealers, prostitutes and their "Johns" inhabited this place. Gone were the families with cute homes and yards with bicycles leaning against mulberry trees.

When I was 15, I used to visit my bio-dad there. He was the proud proprietor of one of the many businesses that sold sex to tourists and locals, alike. Bio-dad ran a stable of about seven girls, all skinny and missing teeth. The girls wore a variety of dirty lingerie meant to entice. When a customer came in, they would prance around and show their wares. Smile, touch a breast, make a date. Bio-dad sat close to protect his assets by any means necessary.

When I was 15, bio-dad asked me to work for him. He tried to sell me the glamour and the money, but I knew better. One look at the other girls and I knew he was full of shit.

That was the first time I had the courage to say "no." I said no to a man who had already killed someone for their refusal of him. I said no to a man who had spent the better part of my life raping and torturing me. I said no.

When I was 15, my life changed.

Chapter Three:
That's Just Crazy!

There have been many times in my life that I've felt completely and utterly insane. My days were pretty normal; go to work, cook dinner for the family, talk on the phone, etc., but on the inside, I was a walking bag of nuts. I didn't hear voices telling me to kill the neighbors' cat, or anything like that. It was more like I was all alone in my head and no one knew. I realize that statement sounds pretty insane in its own right, but it's the only way I know to explain the "crazy" I felt. I would go through each day with normality, but my thoughts were constantly preoccupied with my self-diagnosed insanity. I was sure everyone around me could see how crazy I was, but were too afraid to say anything.

One day in particular was especially bad. I didn't know exactly what was wrong with me, but I was completely out of control, pacing back and forth, and unable to express what was going on inside my head. I felt like a ball of yarn, unraveling as some really mean, fucked up cat batted me back and forth across the room. I didn't know what to do, but I knew I had to do something.

I spent the entire day on the phone, trying to find a therapist who would see me even though I had no insurance, no state assistance, and no money. Finally, by the grace of God, I found a therapist named Michael who agreed to see me at 7:30 that evening.

When I arrived at his office, I told him about my frantic day. I then explained how it felt as if I were floating above the world, watching my life happen to me, instead of actually participating in it. I told him about my reoccurring dreams of flying along, seeing beautiful blue streams and lush fields of green, feeling peaceful and free, when suddenly I was flying really fast and out of control, heading towards power lines and mountains, ultimately to my death, before jolting awake.

Michael let me ramble on and on, then asked me if I had ever been molested as a child. My response was, "Yeah, but that doesn't have anything to do with this." He explained that everything I described to him were classic symptoms of someone who had been abused; the disconnected feeling, the dreams, the feelings of insanity, all of it. I can't tell you what a fucking relief that was to hear! Finally, I was able to put a label on the crazy feelings I had for so long.

I sat in the chair and cried for what seemed like an eternity. I was so happy that I wasn't ready for the loony-bin and that, through therapy, I would be able to get through those rough times a little more easily.

Over the years, I've been through a lot of therapy. Usually, it took months for me to garner the courage to pick up the phone and call for an appointment. I would make all types of excuses to get out of doing what I knew was good for me: I couldn't afford it, I didn't have time, my kids needed new shoes, I just started a new job, etc. Really, I was just afraid of reliving the pain of the abuse. When I finally made the call, the fear was gone and was replaced by kind people who sincerely wanted to help, and each therapist helped me with a different aspect of my recovery.

My therapists gently guided me through the events I could remember, and assisted me in remembering things I just wanted to forget. They helped me identify and face my fears, and learn new ways to cope before moving onto the next phase of my therapy. It was often hard to get through, but was also necessary in the healing process...

Fighting the blues

Fri, 13 Aug 2004

Lately, I've been more depressed than I can remember in a long time. I'm not sure where it's coming from. Yes I have a great deal of stress in my life right now, but it doesn't seem any more intense than I've had before. I just can't seem to shake it.

I haven't had sex in a while now. I usually deal with my stress by calling every guy I know and having meaningless sex with a different guy every day. I haven't done that this time. Maybe that's why it's hard for me to shake; I am dealing with it differently and my brain is freaking out from the lack of endorphins. Hmm...

I just have so many decisions to make right now and I'm so depressed that I'm refusing to answer my phone, I sleep constantly, I've essentially cut off all contact with everyone except Guido. I always have such great advice for everyone else but I can't seem to make myself hear it. They say that you teach what you need to learn yourself.

Seriously, the more I write the more I want to revert to the old way and just make a booty call right now. I think I'll go to sleep instead.

Depression, Sadness.....

Sun, 29 Aug 2004

Fuck it. I give up. I can't stand this fucking depression anymore. Sleep is all I need.

Fuck this.

The painted hand

Thu, 02 Sep 2004

There was a time while I was in counseling that my psychologist taught me about art therapy. She said that if you put paper and pencil in front of you and just draw what you feel, it will sometimes help you remember, sometimes help you heal. Because I've always been artistic, I thought it would be a good idea to try.

I bought a sketch pad and some colored pencils and sat at my kitchen table. My (ex) husband was working out of town and the kids were asleep so I was free to let my mind wander. I remember feeling afraid of the instruments in front of me. I hesitated at the pad again then I picked up the first pencil. I think I chose red.

My drawing started with a straight line, then another and another. I kept switching colors and before I knew it, there was a man's hand before me; fingers with dirty nails and hair on the knuckles. I can't get the image of his hand out of my head, even today. I remember looking at the drawing and wanting to vomit but instead, I went completely numb. I was sitting there at my kitchen table and it's like my "feelings" took over my body. I had no real control of my own hand, I couldn't see, and I was numb from head to toe.

I came out of my "trance" when my daughter got out of bed and touched my arm and scared the shit out of me. After I put her back to bed I studied what I had drawn. On the page was the hand and the words "no," "stop," and "I'm a child!" written over and over in a childlike writing. On top of that I drew drops of blood and swirls. Creepy.

It was amazing to me that my body went into a sort of self-hypnosis while drawing that picture. My subconscious took over and put to paper things I was afraid to see in my conscious mind. I haven't done the drawing exercise since then but I have done some sculpture work, which was less traumatic for me.

Arrested development defined...

Wed, 15 Sep 2004

A few years ago, I was told by my psychologist that I suffer from "arrested development." He told me that when a child suffers a traumatic event their psychosexual / psychosocial development is stopped (or arrested) at the age in which the trauma occurred. So if a child is molested at the age of seven, their development in relation to their maturity, ability to handle difficult situations, sexual self, etc. is halted. The traumatic event causes the normal developmental stages of the child to stop. I'm unclear as to when or how the problem starts to correct itself or how long it takes to become "normal" again, if ever.

I've been thinking about that a lot lately. Although I'm a grown woman, I sometimes feel like a little girl. It's like I don't quite know how to handle situations that come up or I handle them with rash decisions that I regret later. Hell, I'm still learning things I should have known 20 years ago. I guess some of it may come from my memory loss but I've been dealing with that so long, I've learned to recognize when I have no memory vs. things or processes that were never learned to begin with. It's very frustrating sometimes.

It also makes me feel like I'm psychotic or something. It's weird to walk around all the time feeling like everyone else in the world is entirely sane and would certainly never handle a situation like I do. I know it's not true, but it sure feels like it sometimes. I'm also afraid that if anyone ever saw the "real me" they would run screaming. Another fear is that I may not like what I may see in myself. That's probably why I'm having a hard time making a commitment to anyone or anything. Shit! I'm so fucked!

I'm on a mission though. I am going to try to identify the situations that cause me the most angst in these areas then I will try to come up some sort of reasonable fix that will help me stop feeling like a freaking psychotic idiot. I'm also going to try to open myself up a little more. I'm very extroverted now but I think it's probably mostly on a superficial level. I want to be whole.

Introspection

Thu, 25 Nov 2004

Looking in the mirror, I see a face of worry. The deep furrow between my brows shows years of sorrow manifested there. My eyes are kind but void of trust, especially with strangers. High cheekbones reveal my Cherokee heritage. Proud. Warrior. Woman. I like to see my nose as aristocratic, but I'm not sure it's an accurate description. My lips are full and soft, turned down slightly at the sides. I've been told my smile is inviting and friendly. I have a freckle below my bottom lip, halfway to my chin. My hair is thick, long, black, and wavy. I have a lot of hair. I've been told I'm pretty, with an exotic look about me. I have no visible scars, only those on the inside, which can't be seen.

Depression is so damned depressing!
Fri, 03 Dec 2004

Insane is the word I use to describe myself. I'm not clinically insane but sometimes I feel as if my head is going to burst from stress, which of course, *drives* me insane.

It's like I have several, very small, people inside my head and none of them can figure out what the hell to do, so instead, they dance around and cry and shout and laugh and scream at their lack of direction. Can't one of you just make a fucking decision already?! It's frustrating.

Maybe what I really have is the "people pleasers" disease. All of these little people are trying, in vain, to please everyone around them but doing nothing for themselves so they can heal. Maybe they should just take the time to deal with the issues at hand instead of closing their eyes and bumbling and stumbling around on my grey matter.

A welcome place to stay
Sat, 29 Jan 2005

I find myself living deeper and deeper inside my head. It's not really a safe place for me to be, but it's familiar and strangely comforting. I recognize the thoughts there because they've been with me so long. I recognize the fear there because it's been my safety and my guard. I'm afraid and I need to get some help.

The effects of sexual abuse
Sun, 30 Jan 2005

I remember the days when I felt pretty good - confident, intelligent, worthy, and mostly sane. Something's happened in the last few months to make the "pretty good" feeling go away. I'm not that person anymore. Now I'm that person who walks around looking weak and insane and makes you want to cross the street when you see them approaching. At least that's the way I perceive myself to be.

I've recognized the "symptoms" for some time now, but have tried to fight against them. I've been having small flashbacks, elevated fear, and delusional thinking. It happens about every ten years or so. I get counseling, get my head back on straight then forge ahead. Jump forward ten years and there I am, back in with a counselor for my "tune up" so I can start the process all over again.

You may be thinking, "Damn, she's fucking insane," but I assure you it's the by-product of the sexual abuse I suffered as a child. This is what happens, in varying degrees, to people who have been abused. As adults, we have a hard time coping with all the stress, the memories, the feelings of insanity, worthlessness, etc., etc. Some of us, like me, put on a "pretenders" mask and go about life as if we are the most capable people on the planet. What's really happening inside is that we're moving farther and farther away from ourselves - so far that we forget who we really are. Others hide in their homes, afraid to venture out for fear of the world seeing their helplessness and shame, while others hide their fear and shame by drinking or using drugs. The coping mechanisms are all different, depending on who the victim/ survivor is and how much stress they can handle, but the affects are the same.

It's taken me a long time to recognize the warning signs, but I'm glad I do. It doesn't mean that I heed those warnings right away, just that I can see them and know I have to do something. What stops me is the pain of reliving the memories of the abuse. It's a pain so unbearable, like being stabbed then squeezing lemon juice in the stab wounds then being burned in the same spot. It takes a great deal of strength to voluntarily go through it again and again. But, I have to do it - I have two children to think of.

So, yeah I'll get that counseling I need so badly. I don't have insurance right now so I'll need to find a place that will take me on a sliding-fee. The problem is going to be finding a clinic that can get me in right away instead of the usual six month waiting period - I don't think I'll make it that long.

Healing winds
Sat, 08 Jan 2005
My strength is in the wind
Brining to me words
And wisdom

Standing still
Face to the sky
Arms spread wide
Ready to accept what comes

The wind blows through me
Giving me light, knowledge
And strength

In its passage,
the wind takes with it
My fear, my pain
And my weakness

The winds of change
Blow sweet upon
This shattered soul
Bringing courage
Healing
And a strength once hidden

Wake me from my slumber
Sat, 08 Oct 2005

The last time I wrote, I talked about my own despair and my thoughts of suicide. That night, a couple of interesting things happened...

First, I called a local helpline because I knew I needed to talk to someone about the feelings running through me. I didn't want to become another statistic and knew I needed immediate intervention in order to save my life. I dialed the phone and was greeted by a woman named Donna. I started to cry and told her that I needed help. We talked for about a minute when she said, "Do you have thoughts of hurting yourself?" I said, "Yes, all day long." Donna, a therapist with years of experience dealing with potential suicide victims, said to me, "Can you hold on a second?" And without waiting for an answer or the sound of a gunshot to my head, she promptly put me on hold. I was stunned. When she came back on the line, she said, "So you were asking me something..." I hung up.

The funny thing is, me and my twin have this little joke... I call and he answers the phone by saying, "Suicide helpline. Please hold." We laugh at the absurdity of it and go on with our conversation. I couldn't believe the bitch put me on hold, but really couldn't believe that our little joke actually came true. If I was a weaker person, I would have pulled the trigger as soon as Donna came back on the line, just to haunt her for the remainder of her days on earth. Luckily, I don't own a gun and decided that a good nights' sleep might be good for my mental health.

Needless to say, I am feeling better, little by little. The events of the evening taught me a lot about myself. I know that I am stronger than I give myself credit for. I know that I love my children more than I hate myself. I know that I need to get some real help. I know that I need to get back into counseling and get rid of some of the shit that's polluting my mind.

I will be fine. By the grace of God, I will be fine.

I'm about an inch from losing my mind...

Tue, 01 Nov 2005

There's so much wrong with me.

And so much wrong with everyone else.

It's driving me crazy.

Almost quite literally.

I'd try to explain,

but it would take weeks.

I really don't have time

And who would care.

It's in my head

Sun, 11 Dec 2005

What is it? What is that thing in my head that tells me I'm not good enough, not pretty enough, and not worthy of anything, especially love? Why do I continue to believe the negative thoughts in my head? And where did they come from?

I could sit here all day long and tell you why YOU are a magnificent person. I can see inside your soul and find the beauty there. Why can't I see what's looking at me in the mirror? Why can't I believe the truths people see in me?

Every so often good thoughts come through, but then I feel as if I need validation to actually believe them. It's as if I'm a great pretender, projecting to you what I *think* you want to see, while actually believing something completely different.

The funny thing is I know that my heart feels good. I know that what I'm feeling is truly "all in my head." I am my own worst enemy.

Reprogramming my thought process has been an objective of mine for years now. Had you seen me 10-15 years ago, you would have seen a completely different person, so I guess it's worked a bit.

What just hit me is that I'm not being completely honest with myself. I'm not being honest about my own faults or short-comings for fear that you'll see them too. If I were completely honest about these things, I could make a decision to change or accept them. The trouble is, I'm not sure what the actual faults are, and what was put in my head years ago that isn't true at all. Well, maybe it *was* true years ago but isn't now. Hm. Pondering.

So what do I do? Should I sit and make a list of all the things I see as "wrong" about me? Then make a list of all the good? Would that really solve anything? Or am I letting fear get in the way?

How the hell do I start loving me again?

Chapter Four: Memory... The Good, the Bad, and the Ugly

Until the age of 28, I believed that, as a child, there was a man who lived in the attic of my childhood home. In my mind, I believed the man would come down at night and sit in the little chair by my door and watch me sleep. I imagined that during the day, while my family was gone, he would come downstairs, make a bologna sandwich for lunch and make himself at home. Several times as an adult, I reminded my brother about the man and he always said he didn't remember him. My brother remembers everything that went on in our childhood and I remember almost nothing, but I didn't think much of his lack of memory in this instance.

Years later, while in a group counseling session, another woman in the group was telling her story when I flashed back to the man who lived in the attic, and suddenly realized it was all a lie. The truth was that the man was one of my abusers and the whole story was a threat they used to keep me quiet. I had been told that I was always being watched and that they would know if I told anyone our "secret." When I realized that I had re-invented the threat into something my mind could manage, it made me feel foolish and ashamed.

After I cried what seemed like a river of tears, my emotions changed and I was angrier than I could ever remember. My abusers had fucked with my mind and completely shifted my perception of who I was. No longer could I count on what I "remembered" as being real; instead, I had to reevaluate everything about my life and question every previous memory, including the few good memories I had cherished before. At that moment, it felt as if my entire life was a lie, and if my life were a lie, I rationalized, maybe I had fooled myself into *believing* I was abused when I wasn't. That's where my mind went, and it made me angry as hell.

Most of my life memories are made up of bits and pieces, or flashes, of memory. I remember faces, mostly, but I don't remember events or conversations that have taken place; I just don't remember being there, wherever there is.

My new memories are like snapshots, really. When a friend or family members tells a story about some party or family get-together, I can remember the faces of the people there, and I may remember what a place looks like, but I have no memory of being there or being part of the event. As the story progresses, I take the faces of the people involved, add it to the place I'm being told about, then add a "picture" of myself there, and that becomes my new memory. See, most of my memories are not my own, but a culmination of stories and snapshots that belong to other people.

It's been difficult to go through life hearing funny stories about this or that, and have no idea what the other person is talking about, and that makes every one of my real memories precious to me. When I realized that the man in the attic was not a real memory, it almost destroyed me.

Becoming vulnerable

Sun, 21 Nov 2004

I've been sitting at this keyboard for some time now, trying to figure out what to write. I have so much in my head but I'm not sure what to say. I'm angry, and sad, and depressed, and frustrated, and lonely, and afraid. I'm also hopeful that things will be okay.

I need to deal with my hidden pain. It's hard to describe, but it's as if I am 100 different people all trapped in the same body. No, I don't have multiple personalities. I have just always felt as if I NEEDED to be 100 different people just to make it through life. I don't know who I am anymore.

When I look in the mirror, it's not me I see. I see some other woman "pretending" to be me; the face I've borrowed for the day. Sometimes I think I see glimpses of me, but I'm not really sure. Sometimes the me I see is ugly and angry and evil and mean. Sometimes the me I see is pretty and sexy and confident and kind. I truly have no idea if any of those images is me at all; maybe they are and I'm choosing to ignore them. Maybe I'm seeing parts of myself that I don't like and those are the traits I need to change.

I also know that my memories may be too painful to bear and that's why they are lost. My cousin once said that she didn't even remember me being around for family functions, etc. even though the photographs show me there. She said that maybe God was carrying me then because I couldn't walk alone. It's very comforting for me to believe that.

I'm not sure where to go from here. How do I find out who I really am? And what if I don't like the person I see? It's all so scary but so necessary. I can't keep living this life and feeling as if it's all a big lie. I need to find myself and my meaning in life.

I am not a victim. I am a survivor.

Flashbacks from hell

Fri, 17 Dec 2004

There was a time in my life, when on a regular basis I experienced "flashbacks" of my abuse. Mostly they occurred during sex, but not always. Sometimes I would flashback because I walked near a man who happened to be wearing the same cologne as my bio-dad. The familiar scent would take me back to those horrible days and nights when he used me for his pleasure. The scent lingers in my memory, haunting me and assaulting my senses. Other times, it took only a laugh, a word, or the shape of someone's mouth to take me back to those times.

To live it once is bad enough, to live it again is excruciating. I know that flashbacks are a means of helping the adult deal with the emotional affects of childhood abuse, but in a grown up way, using grown up coping mechanisms. It sounds good in theory. What I know is the pain. I know the feeling of blacking out during a flashback then finding myself huddled in the corner of my closet, hiding myself in the clothes, a lighter in my hand. I remember thinking that everything would be okay if I could just "burn away the demons." There were times when it felt as if I were literally shrinking, becoming that small child again, vulnerable to the wants of the "loving" adults around me. Sometimes I screamed - the scream of someone trying to exorcise their demons - the scream of someone who's being ripped apart piece by piece, their flesh being torn from their body then thrown into a vat of acid - the scream that no one heard.

So intense was the emotional pain that I felt the need to redirect it by causing myself physical pain. I would pound myself in the head with my fist to stop the memories from invading anymore space. I would claw my face to bleeding to erase the ugly I saw there. I held my body under scalding hot showers to cleanse myself of the disgust that was me. I hurt. What's odd is that I bear no physical scars from the damage I inflicted upon myself. Of course, I still bear the emotional scars that no one, but myself, can see.

My flashbacks nearly stopped almost completely over ten years ago when my bio-dad was in the hospital and almost died. I saw in him as an old and frail man who was unable to hurt me anymore…

A shift of balance
Sun, 26 Dec 2004
Shifting, changing
moving, running
in slow motion
to a place unseen

Cold, snow
white hills
trees hiding for the winter
people hiding from themselves

Black to red
black and blue
babies bundled
A bag of things

Fear, exhilaration
Terror, paranoia
looking over your shoulder
for someone unseen

Red brick building
security doors
worried faces
reach out a hand
Eyes of blue
shifting and changing
seeing a future
without pain

It's a peaceful place I like to call denial

Thu, 14 Apr 2005

On the surface denial is a beautiful place with fields of yellow wildflowers, tall oaks, and singing birds. While in denial you walk with a slight lift in your step, arms outstretched, welcoming all the wonderful people who stop in to say hello. Denial is replete with quaint little shops selling exquisite wares and coffee shops that serve exotic blends. Denial is divine... until you look just beyond the ridge and your eyes see the land of reality.

Suddenly, denial isn't such a happy place. The wildflowers are replaced with weeds, the trees are dying, and the birds have flown away. Denial becomes dark and dingy. The ground seems to be made of some weird sticky substance that is holding your feet down and making it nearly impossible to walk. The wonderful people of denial are transformed into gargoyles and monsters who grab at your soul. The shops become sex clubs and the once aromatic coffee becomes bitter on your tongue as reality beckons you closer.

I can see reality now - it's over there, just at the edge of the horizon. The sun is rising with brilliance, warming me and unleashing my ties. If I can just hold on a bit longer, trudge through the weeds and the pain, get past the monsters who are trying to pull me back, then I might just make it.

Right now everything is calm. The nightmares have stopped, the flashbacks are becoming fewer, and my mood appears to have lifted a bit. Yes, I'm still in the land of denial but reaching towards reality.

Yet another epiphany... and this one's good

Sat, 18 Jun 2005

There's so much going on in my head that I'm not quite sure where to start....

I've always had a problem having sex in the missionary position. I've always attributed it to the weight of the man on me and how it sent me into flashbacks of when dear ol' bio-dad molested me. At the age of three, or five, or seven the weight of a full-grown man is crushing. Now, it feels as if I can't breathe and my shoulders feel as if they're on fire. I've tried over the years to deal with it by reminding myself that I'm now an adult who is making a conscious choice to have sex, but it's still difficult at times. Usually, I just choose to not have missionary-style sex.

Tonight, while with my guy, he was on top and we were both being very quite because my daughter is home (I certainly don't want her to know what mommy is doing in the bedroom). Anyway, he's on top, my shoulders are on fire, I can't breathe, AND I'm trying to be very quiet. It was then that I realized it was exactly like that when bio-dad abused me. I wasn't allowed to move or scream. I just had to lay there, with the full weight of him on me, and take it. Tonight, it felt the same. No, it wasn't as if my guy was abusing me, it's just that I was in full flashback mode.

I never put together the reason I am now very vocal while having sex and not liking the missionary position. It's as if the abuse is being replayed every time. It's unreal to me that's it's taken me so long to recognize that exact scenario. It may not be the best "memory" to have but it's useful in my recovery.

Sneakin` and Creepin`

Wed, 11 Jan 2006

Last night I had the opportunity to get a full eight hours of sleep. I settled into my oh-so-wonderful and comfortable bed and immediately fell asleep. About four hours later, my daughter quietly came into my room and I woke up. I asked what she was doing and she explained that she needed some nail clippers. That's cool. Problem is, I couldn't shake the "sneakin' and creepin'" feeling it brought.

For the next four hours, I lay in bed, partially awake and trying to shake the feeling. I was exhausted and my body kept fighting for sleep while my mind was fighting to stay awake. I did sleep again but it wasn't restful at all. I kept waiting for someone to come creepin' into my room again. When I got up this morning, I was in a terrible mood - fucked up because my sleep was so fucked up. After about half an hour, I finally figured out why I couldn't sleep after my daughter came into my room last night.

When bio-dad sexually abused me, he used to tell me that he was always watching me. I believed that his friend (the man behind the camera) came into my bedroom every night and watched me sleep. I believed there was a hole in my wall where bio-dad could see me. He told me that he'd kill my mom, my brothers, and me if I told anyone what they were doing. I was a small child and believed them.

So last night, when my daughter came into my room, it brought back that feeling of being watched. It brought back some of those old feelings of not being safe and being taken advantage of. Fucking creepy.

At least I understand where it came from and can deal with the emotions of it while I'm awake. Definitely creepy though.

Chapter Five:
Fighting Sexual Addiction

I've cheated with a married man, put myself in too many dangerous situations to even count, and have done a lot of idiotic things I'm not proud of today. At the time I thought little of my behavior, because I thought little of myself. I felt worthless and that I deserved whatever I got.

As I was in the midst of my addiction, there was a part of me that knew what I was doing was wrong, but felt helpless to stop because the rush of it was so intoxicating. What kept the addiction alive was the need to feel human, to feel loved, and to feel wanted. Mostly, I just wanted to feel like I mattered to someone.

Looking back, I realize the absurdity of it all, but it's where I was at the time.

Horny and proud!
Mon, 04 Oct 2004
Yesterday was pure hell for me. I was so fucking horny I couldn't even stand myself. Every uttered word, every action made

me want to rip the clothes off almost any guy available and just fuck him like a crazy person! What made things worse is that I got a call from almost every "sex friend" I have - one even begged me to come over. He promised additional sexual favors in return. I said no to them all. I'm so proud of myself.

Believe me, I really wanted to go and any of them would have been fine. I just needed a good fuck, but for all the wrong reasons. I told the beggar that I was not going to have meaningless sex anymore and that even though we've known each other (and have been having sex) for almost a year, neither of us really gave a shit about the other. It was only about the sex and I just wasn't going to go there anymore. He kept promising more sex tricks and begging me to go, but I held my resolve and damn it felt good.

The only reason I really wanted to have sex so bad is because of my date with "nice guy" on Saturday night. He really seems like a very normal guy... he's respectful, romantic, intelligent, nice looking, doesn't abuse any substances, has a great job, and is a good parent. Absolutely no chaos! That's probably what's driving me to sex. I'm so used to dating guys with problems and drama that when a nice guy comes along, I don't have a clue what to do. And of course, the first thing I think to do is to have crazy meaningless sex with chaotic guys.

Anyway, I'm proud of myself for not giving in. It was hard but it did it. Thank God my friend Guido was there to help talk me down and to tell me how proud she is of me. That helped a lot... along with the pacing, biting my nails, pacing some more, I think my head spun around a couple of times too.

Oh, I almost forgot. The last thing I saw last night before going to bed was Brad Pitt in Fight Club. That man is smokin' fuckin' hot dude! Thank God he's married to Jennifer or I'd be all over his shit!

I`m gonna knit a big fat dildo and have some cotton love.
Sun, 10 Oct 2004

I'm having a hard time today with my sexual addiction. No, I haven't done the dirty deed, but I want to. I want to call one of my guys and just get freaky. No, I won't but dammit, it's been four weeks! The strange thing about all of it is that I am really horny but my attitude has shifted so much that I'm not willing to just have sex for that reason alone. Sex has to mean something for me now.

This is probably coming on because I had a lunch date with a REALLY boring guy today. It was our second date. The first date was fine but I did want to stick a fork in my eye about half way through the date. I attributed it to my severe lack of nicotine so I was trying to give it another try. We met at the park so we could just sit and talk. He's a nice guy but hasn't had any adventure or excitement in his life. I'm like, "shit, no drama or chaos is great, but fuck, could you at least have a little bit of personality?" When I left the park I wanted to make a couple of calls and go fuck the shit out of someone who actually DOES have a personality. Anyone!

I left the park and went to meet a client (whom I've slept with once before). He's a very animated person, talking with his hands like he's signing. Everything was fine until he started making this gesture which was totally turning me on. I had to ask him to stop. He understood the effect it was having on me so he stopped and smiled slyly at me. Asshole. We only had sex once but definitely still have a chemistry. We also have a very good friendship so we won't be doin' the nasty again. Argh! I hate feeling like this but am so proud of myself for not giving in.

On a lighter note, I learned how to change the spark plugs in my car today. Thank God it's finally running better and I'm not afraid of pulling out into traffic and killing everyone in my car. Maybe I'll take up mechanics in order to get control of my addiction. I'll be the sexiest fucking mechanic in town. Shit, then the guys would be lining up wanting me to work on their cars, pulling out their big tools and offering em' up to me. Shit, maybe I'll just take up knitting.

The devil's at my doorstep

Thu, 14 Oct 2004

So, just when I think I'm really doing well with my sexual addiction, I start getting offer after offer to have meaningless sex. Suddenly the porn sites start popping up on my monitor and people are offering me cybersex and phone sex. The shit is all around me!

I'll admit that I've been dabbling with the cyber and phone stuff but haven't had "bumpin' uglies" sex with anyone in over four weeks. I do know that I need to stop the other stuff too though. I feel it's weakening my resolve to stay my course.

I'm afraid though. Afraid that if I stop sex all-together I'll be reluctant to start again, even when the right guy comes along. I'm afraid that I'll become a-sexual and never want it again. Maybe that's foolish, but it's something that crosses my mind.

I guess maybe I'm really afraid that I was just pretending to like sex. I'm afraid of losing the feeling of exhilaration and excitement and depravity of some of the things I've done. I feel sick just saying it. I never want to be my bio-dad. It's like the kinkier I get, the more like him I become. No, I have never and would never have sex with a child, like he did me, but I'm so afraid of becoming as sick as him. He helped in my creation; does that mean I'll be like him? It's fucking scary to even think about. He has hurt so many people and I never want to do that. I guess I just continue hurting myself instead. Whoa. Epiphany.

I know I'm on the right track but it's so fucking hard. Bio-dad was/is the most evil man I've ever known. He just takes the life of a child and destroys it without any thought. I'll bet his shoes meant more to him than any of the human beings he hurt.

All I can hope is that he gets his punishment in the end. I know God is a loving God, but I can't imagine God loving that. Sounds more like the devils handiwork than anything. I do feel sorry for bio-dad, in a way. I can't imagine putting so many people through so much hell and liking yourself. I think he's in a hell all his own.

I think I was a man in a previous life... just an observation
Wed, 20 Oct 2004

I'm perplexed. It seems the relationship I continually have with men is one that can be described only as "dude (that's me), you're the best friend I ever had. Would you suck my dick?"

Having male friends is a great thing but I'm really sick of them hitting on me (and me giving in occasionally) then telling me about the "real" dates they've recently gone on with the

20-year-old model who is drop-dead gorgeous. Um, hello! I'm pretty fucking hot myself. Okay, not drop-dead, but man, do I have to hear all the details? I know, I know, that's what friends do - they go into detail. But I think once WE have done the dirty, then rule #2 goes into effect... no telling the person you JUST slept with about the girl you WANT to sleep with. Oy!

I'm not really irritated; I just think it's funny. My male friends are attracted to me but want to remain friends. I've been told that there is something about me that's "comforting" and "it's like talking to an old friend." I'm happy that I provide that to these men, but my ego gets slightly bruised when the talk turns to sex... with others. I'm not complaining. I would rather be friendly and have the opportunity to meet the people I do than act in the reverse. I like the fact that I'm outgoing and that people trust me with their thoughts. I guess things could be worse.

Kisses and Hugs!

Mr. Pretty keeps knocking at my door!
Mon, 25 Oct 2004

I'm doing so well then "Mr. Pretty" calls and wants to hook up. Man oh man! I am so tempted - he really does have the prettiest dick I've ever seen. Can I break my rules just once?

Sex! Sex! Sex!
Thu, 28 Oct 2004

I gave in to "Mr. Pretty." I won't go into detail. All I can say is...

WHY THE HELL WAS I GIVING UP ON SEX?
THAT SHIT'S GOOD!

I do have a better understanding of the reasons why I was trying to not have sex. I know that rotating sex amongst my five guys (not at the same time) was not a good thing for me, mentally. I know that it felt great and powerful when I was in the moment, but it felt bad and dirty the next day. I know that I need to have an emotional connection to someone if I'm going to have sex with him; that wasn't the case with the other guys. Now I just have to reevaluate the situation and find that balance between the two. I do want to continue to have sex, but it has to be with the right guy and not just for the sake of doing it.

This was a healthy experience for me. I gave in and crossed the line, I don't feel bad, it's giving me reflection, and I want to stay balanced. I do feel as if I've made another step forward.

Three cheers for Mr. Pretty!
Mon, 29 Nov 2004

I'm trying to find my balance between meaningless sex and sex that's fulfilling with someone I care for. What I've been doing, however, is fighting hard against having any sex at all, which is not healthy either. At the risk of sounding like a complete slut, I did have six guys I could call for sex anytime I wanted, but I've cut the list down to three. The ones I eliminated are the guys who were as horny as me and would fuck all day if I agreed. Now on my list are the guys who understand sexual balance and respect my need for that balance.

One of the guys I kept on my list is Mr. Pretty. We've talked about my issues quite a bit lately and he understands my need to make a change in our arrangement. I'm really happy about that because Mr. Pretty is the one man I've had the most difficult time resisting. He's ultra sexy, hard-bodied, skin like milk chocolate, and has the prettiest dick I've ever seen. Yeah, I know I've written about him before, but DAMN that man is F.I.N.E. Everything about him is fine, including his intelligence and sense of humor. I'm just glad I get to swing in his playground every so often. (Don't worry, protection is ALWAYS included.)

I hooked up with Mr. Pretty today and had a deliciously wonderful time. What was so great is the fact that I didn't feel "weird" afterwards, as has happened in the past. By rewiring my thoughts on sex, I was able to just go with the flow and have a good time. No self-inflicted head games. No problems.

It's so curious to me the things we do to ourselves. I could sit here and play a bunch of negative shit in my head but it wouldn't get me anywhere. I'm proud of the progress I've made so far. It may not be what others would choose, but it's an okay choice for me at this point. And the best part is that I can change my rules and my "balance" as I go. Nothing's set in stone.

Sometimes I just need a slap in the head to FINALLY get it!
Thu, 09 Dec 2004

Right before Easter last year, I dated a guy named John. We only went out a few times but did have a good connection. We shared artistic interests, tastes in food, language, culture, humor, and the like. We seemed to have a good start on our dating relationship.

I left town to visit a friend over the Easter holiday but called John when I returned. I didn't get a call back. I tried one more time, but still no return call. I wasn't sure what happened, but I was sure he didn't want to see me again. Sometimes these things happen without explanation. Whatever. Yes, I was a little butt-hurt, but we hadn't become so close that it devastated me.

A couple of days ago, guess who calls me? Yep, John. He explained that he had lost my phone number and really wanted to get in touch and was so excited to be talking to me and blah, blah, blah. We talked for a while about what we've been doing, work, kids, life. It was a nice conversation. He then asked if he could come over to see me sometime over the weekend, I said sure, and we made tentative plans. Great. John called later that evening and, again, exclaimed his joy at having found me again. You see, he missed me so much, thought about me often, and most of all, he missed the sex! Okay, what the fuck? Thank you for being an asshole and reducing me to my skill in the sack. That's when the epiphany hit.

I realized that the labels we put on ourselves are actually self-fulfilling prophecies and only serve to perpetuate the negative thoughts we all carry around. I've been calling myself a sex addict because I say I'm addicted to sex. In actuality, I'm addicted to the euphoric responses I get *during* sex. It's not the act alone, it's the release of endorphins that fuels me. I like the "happy rush" I get. That's the "drug" I'm addicted to.

I can't believe it took me so long to figure it out when you all have been saying it all along. Okay, maybe I have a "skill" but I don't have to be labeled by it. I would much rather walk around with the label of "friend" or "caring" or "intelligent." I was so angry about his comments and ashamed that I'd held onto the label all this time. Today is a new day. No longer will I carry around a label that does nothing but bring shame and disgust to my soul. Today I start anew. Aren't epiphanies great?

73

Trust, love, and meaningless sex
Sat, 05 Feb 2005

I think that maybe I shouldn't post all the thoughts running around in my head. The more I write, I'm discovering, the more I sound like a freakin' lunatic.

The thoughts sound good "in my head," but not so much when actually written down. Yes, I love two different men, but the real point is my propensity to run away when anyone gets too close to me. Now that G has used the L-word, I want to run for the hills. And because A-man is just as afraid of commitment as I am, he seems like the safer bet. Love really has nothing to do with any of it. I like to kid myself into believing that it does, but in reality, it's all about me being scared and chasing what can't be caught (and lives at least 1,000 miles away). It's something I'm working on, but still having a hard time with.

My problem is that I've been used and abused so much in the past that it's difficult for me to trust anyone with my heart. I do pray that someday I'll be able to get over the past so I can deal with the present and the future. I want to "feel" again, but it's just such a foreign concept to me. I guess that's why meaningless sex has been so appealing; I don't have to worry about getting hurt. When you go into it with the knowledge that they don't want a relationship anymore than you do, it's make it easy to do. And safe.

I am making progress though. There is only one guy who I will continue having meaningless sex with (as opposed to the six I had available to me before), I have found a counselor who will see me for a reduced fee, and I am trying, very hard, to open myself up to the potential pain (and joy) of a relationship. I'm taking baby-steps here.

I may write more lunatic-laced blather occasionally, but just take it for what it's worth...

Swingers Club Virgin

Fri, 04 Mar 2005

I've always been curious about it, so I went to a swingers club last night with my friend, John. It was everything, and nothing, that I expected.

The club was in a very industrial part of town, the roads leading there were eerily quiet, and the building was very non-descript. We went in, filled out some paperwork, paid our fees, and with much anticipation, walked in to the unknown. Because the men far outnumber the women, all I saw was a sea of testerone eyeing me as if they were starving and I was the catch of the day. It was a welcoming yet creepy feeling. We got a drink (soda only as alcohol is prohibited) and sat down. Our nerves were getting the better of us, so we started chain-smoking immediately. As we sat talking, I looked around and saw one other couple in the room. That brought the totals to two women and ten men.

Within 30 minutes of our arrival, we had sex by ourselves once (in the 70's-style porn den), and were asked by a single guy if he could watch us next time, which we declined. Next we saw a woman take off her blouse and her date sucking her nipples. After a few minutes of that, she got up and took off the shirt of a lone guy on the dance floor. I'm not sure when it happened, but the next thing you know, this guy has his pants off and he's wearing a leopard-print thong. It was not attractive in the least. She went back to her table and the sucking continued while another four guys stood around the table and watched. Turn around again and dancer guy is naked (even more unattractive than before). We got up to walk around the rooms in the back and were followed by five guys, all hoping and praying that we'd get a room and invite one (or all) of them in for the party.

As we were walking around, a staff member asked if we had any questions. We talked with him a bit and I learned so much about swingers clubs:

- Because of the laws and zoning requirements, each room has to be locked after entering.

- There cannot be more than six people in the room at one time. Apparently, seven or more people having sex constitutes a violation of the law

- Towels and condoms are supplied.

- If you have an allergy to bleach, you probably better not get near the towels or sheets, but use a vinyl surface instead

- You can be in any stage of dress (or undress) anywhere in the club, but you cannot have sex while not in a room

- Touching above the waist only while not in a room

- No exchanging sex for favors or money

- No means no

We went back to the table and quite a few more people had arrived. Totals = four women and 20 men. We were approached by another man who wanted to watch us have sex. See, I thought that a swingers club was for people who wanted to HAVE sex with each other, not just watch. So naive. We decided to have sex again and, this time, went to the fishbowl. It's a little strangely exciting to have sex in a room where people know you're having sex and are probably listening at the door.

Since last night, I've had mixed feelings about the experience. On one hand, it's like a paradise for me; I can go and have sex all the time with anyone I want. On the other hand, it's a nightmare; I can go and have sex all the time with anyone I want. After a lot of thought, I think the latter scenario is winning out. I'm sure that having the availability of lots and lots of sex is not a good thing for a sex addict who's trying to heal. Now, because I know this place exists (and I have a year-long membership and can get in for free), I want to run over there tonight and get busy. I want to have sex with a multitude of men and women. I want to get freaky and be free. I want to, but I won't. The temptation is quite overwhelming, I must say, but I will abstain.

I didn't realize, until today, how addicted I am to the wonderful sensations that are sex. I love everything about it. I know that it's my drug just as meth is to an addict. My hope is that my anxious feelings will subside as the days pass. I guess I'll just take it one day at a time.

Just say no!
Sat, 05 Mar 2005
Since my swingers club experience, I've been thinking a lot about my sexual addiction. It seems to have reared its ugly head in a big way. I'm constantly horny and can't shake the sensation. I want sex. Bad.

What I'm struggling with the most is trying to identify what's "normal" <u>for me</u> in regards to sex. I truly don't have any idea. It's like a drug. I want it, I have it, and then I want more and can't get enough. I know what drives me are the feelings I get while having sex. I like the escape, I guess. I like feeling wanted and desired. I like knowing that I please a man. Sex isn't love but it's the closest thing I have right now. And it's pathetic.

My perfect scenario is to be in a committed relationship with a man who is kinky enough to satisfy my appetite, but not an all-out freak. I want to be in that relationship. I want to be with just one man. What I can't seem to do right now is to stop having sex with the men who are currently in my life. I have significantly cut the numbers in the last six months, but I still have a few. I did decide, however, to show John the door; he's definitely not good for me.

So how do I separate normal sex from sex that's not good for me? Sex is a natural part of life and I shouldn't completely deny myself, but where do I draw the line? How the hell do I get there? One thing is for sure, I won't be going back to the club. It really is tempting, but as so many of you have pointed out, I should stay far, far away. I know that it would only serve to dehumanize the whole sexual experience for me. What I really need is to have sex become part of a loving experience instead. With God's help, maybe I'll just get there someday.

My own two feet!
Fri, 11 Mar 2005

This past week has been full of absurdity. Between the swinger's club experience, the naked pictures I've received on email, and all the completely dysfunctional people hitting on me, I finally realized how idiotic my life really is.

Some people want to believe that being a sex addict is days full of eroticism, sensuality, orgasms, and really hot naked people satisfying your every desire. In reality, it's full of depravity, a temporary endorphin rush that leaves you feeling worthless, and self-hate.

No more for me! Starting today, I will abstain from sex. There, I've said it! You know what's going to happen now, don't you? Every sick, depraved, and horny person who's ever wanted to sleep with me, or who I've ever slept with, will suddenly call, begging for a lay. Maybe I'll change my phone number... lol.

Standing on my own two feet sounds pretty good to me.

A View From the Inside
Sun, 13 Mar 2005
Red. The color of anger
Yellow. The color of fear
Black. The color of hatred
The colors will fade
Into my past
Not forgotten
But forgiven
Into a world
Vibrant and warm
Awash with colors anew
And hope.

Coming out in the open

Sun, 03 Apr 2005

Well, I finally did it! I sent a link to G so he can read my journal. I want him to know the "real" me, good and bad. I feel bad because I've lied to him about sleeping with other men, but I sense he didn't really want to hear the truth anyway. The one time I did tell him about another guy it almost broke us apart. I had just fallen in love with him, I was dependent on him, and I didn't want to lose that. I've said it before, G is a good man, it's just that he doesn't know the me shown on these pages. This is who I am. No, I don't like it and that's why I'm trying to change myself; I'm trying to become a better person. I don't know if he'll like the real me, but it's a risk I have to take if I want to move forward.

I am trying very hard to say no to J in regards to the swinger's club. It's so tempting and seems so exciting, but as a friend pointed out, isn't that the nature of addiction? It sounds good in the short-term but isn't so great in the long-term. I have to look to my future and what I'm trying to accomplish with my therapy then make a decision based on that.

Friday was just so rough and I feel as if I'm trying to rebel against the memories and the pain. The old me is saying, "hey, it's just sex and lots of it with anyone I want." The new me is saying, "um, isn't that why you're all fucked up to begin with?" I want to do the right thing, but I'm telling you, it is extremely difficult.

I asked Guido to stay close by her phone in case I need her for support in my efforts to say no. Seriously, who knew it would be so difficult to say that little two-letter word.

Finding my voice

Mon, 04 Apr 2005

A funny thing happened yesterday. For the first time ever, I felt as if I actually had a choice in regards to sex. What an exhilarating experience that was for me! I feel free! What's most incredible is that my voice was actually heard! Believe it or not, I learned this while at the swingers club. Yes, I went after all. Anyway...

When I think of a swingers club, I immediately imagine naked bodies and lost souls trying to find a home. What I found instead were human beings of like-minds, enjoying the company of another, while completely respecting each other's boundaries. In this place, there is no walking up and touching someone just because you want to. If you aren't invited or ask for permission, you simply don't touch. Period. If you say "no," then the answer is no. I know it sounds strange to say I found my voice in such a place, but it really did happen.

Think about how many times you've been inside a nightclub, sports bar, etc. and seen someone getting groped or generally harassed by someone who didn't recognize a person's right to say no or to just be left alone. How funny that a swingers club, a place you wouldn't expect to find ethics, actually contains the most respectful people I've ever met. Boundaries are boundaries and you respect those of others. Period.

For the first time, I felt in complete control of my own body, mind, and soul. I've always felt obligated to do what my partner wanted without taking into consideration how it might affect me. I was there to perform, basically. I'm not laying the blame on my partner; it's just that the messages in my head were always telling me I didn't have a choice. What I learned last night is that I do have a choice. I've had the ability to say "no" all along, I just didn't use it.

I learned a great lesson from my experience there. It doesn't mean I'm going back, it just means that I found out something new about myself. I found my voice again and I plan on using it every chance I get.

Over a hump...

Mon, 18 Apr 2005

Saturday night was a little rough. I was bored and horny and tried several things to get my mind off of sex. I chatted with a friend, talked to G for a few minutes, cleaned my kitchen, and did some laundry. When all was said and done, I still wanted human contact (and some dick), so I planned my outing to the swinger's club.

After showering, shaving all the right things, and making myself look all pretty, I got dressed in my silky black skirt and white tank (sans bra), slipped on my sexy new shoes and prepared myself to go. Of course, I was only going with the intent of just sitting at the bar and talking or people watching. I even thought about taking some notes and writing a book about my experiences. That would entail me visiting quite often, so I convinced myself that I could go without actually having sex with anyone. If I wanted to, I could sit there topless, you know, to release some pent up urges, but I didn't have to go any further. Yes, I realize I was only trying to justify going and, intellectually,

I was winning the argument. And anyway, I have a lifetime membership and get in for free, so I can't just let that go to waste.

So my swinger's club excursion went down this way... I got all primped, looked sexy as hell, and ended by me sitting at my computer instead and joining an online addicts group. You heard me right, I didn't go!! Yippee!! All the intellectual bullshit in the world wasn't going to take away the worthlessness I would have felt the next day. Take that sexual addiction!! Ha!

Now, instead of basking in the faux glow of stranger-supplied endorphins, I am patting myself on the back for getting over this little hump and winning the battle. At least for today. I must say that it feels pretty damn good to know that I was tempted but fought the urge and just stayed home. This is a whole new kind of "rush." I think I like it...

Knock knock....
Tue, 19 Apr 2005
Yeah, that's Mr. Pretty knocking at my door. Okay fine, I'll admit it, I actually knocked on *his* door. I was horny as hell and I couldn't take it anymore!

See, Mr. Pretty is the exception to my abstinence rule. He's the exception because I don't feel worthless or weird after I sleep with him. We're friends, we are both sex addicts and we have an understanding - it's all about the sex and that's it. There's no chance of a commitment, no wondering whether we'll get that "day after" phone call, nothing. We're just two horny people helping to satisfy each others' needs. Hell, if a little lunchtime fun with him keeps me out of the swinger's clubs then I'm okay with that. Well, then there's the fact that he does have the prettiest dick I've ever seen. Honestly, it's perfect. Damn, I need to quit thinking about it...

Anyway, I went days without sex and did cross a big hurdle by keeping myself away from the club on Saturday night. That was a big victory for me and I don't consider my tryst today a failure in my journey. It may be that I'm rationalizing this, but sex with Mr. Pretty is different because we have already defined what the relationship is and is not. Get me?

I'm sure that someday I'll get to the point where I don't have sex with him anymore. Right now, it is what it is. Each day I become healthier is another step towards a new beginning with new rules, and luckily, I can change the rules anytime I want.

Clean as a whistle!
Fri, 27 May 2005
The best news for a sex addict is that she's free of all sexually-transmitted diseases. You heard me right! All my tests came back negative! It's never felt so good to be negative! Yeah, I was worried... actually, I said to my friend Guido, "shit man, I'm probably like a walking fucking petrie dish or something!" To which she replied, "Everything will be okay." Of course, in her head she was saying the same as me but didn't voice it. (She's a good friend.) I was worried because although I used condoms during my sexual exploits, shit can happen... condoms can leak or break, hands are going everywhere, mouths are on everything, bodily fluids of all sorts are being exchanged, etc. I was afraid that my past was going to come back to haunt me in a really bad way.

When I got the results, I thanked God about a thousand times for blessing me this way. I've always said that me and God have an agreement; I'm changing my ways and he's keeping the crap off my back and out of my body. Whew!

Now that that's over, I'll continue to deny all the good men of Arizona any lovin' and keep myself clean. This has been a huge wake-up call for me, you know? I've decided to get tested once a year during my annual well-woman exam to make sure nothing sneaked in and is laying dormant.

I want to celebrate by having a nice cold cocktail but I'm not allowed alcohol because of my liver problem. So all of you out there who CAN drink, have one for me. We'll call it the "Kelly's crotch ain't smelly and she ain't gonna die" celebration!

Snake-Eyed Universe - UPDATE! UPDATE!
Thu, 09 Jun 2005

I woke up this morning feeling quite frisky. I mean, really-super-duper-gotta-have-me-some-big-ol-dick horny! I slowly sauntered up to the guy I'm seeing, giving him that come-hither look, then I jumped in his lap and gave him a very passionate kiss. It was the kind of kiss that can bring a man to his knees and make him write bad checks. Then I looked at the clock and realized there wasn't even enough time for a quickie. Shit!

So off to work I went, feelin' all sexy and looking forward to what's sure to come tonight. For a brief moment I thought of Mr. Pretty and how easy it would be to satisfy my urges through meaningless, pussy-pounding sex, then I thought better of it and went on my way.

Well guess what? Apparently the smell of my lust can reach far and wide because not only did Mr. Pretty call today, but so did all of my other former fuck buddies. It's as if the universe stuck its face between my legs, took a lick, and breathed the scent out to those in my past. Weird. I ignored the calls, by the way. I stuck to my guns and am just waiting for the daily grind to end so I can do the nightly grind with my guy.

Fucking snake-eyed universe anyway.... hmpf.

Update! The horn-dogs were still on the prowl today but I was able to fight them off using my powers of honesty and integrity. The people I was most honest with was my guy, and myself. I told him about the calls and let him know that I needed his help. Get this... he didn't get mad. He didn't run. He stood by me through the rough patch. I think I may have found a keeper. What I realized is that it would be easy for me to do a "quick lunch" with Mr. Pretty and my guy would never know. At the same time, it would be easy for my guy to get back into his addiction and I would never know. I wouldn't like that anymore than he would like me fucking someone else. I'd have to say I've learned some pretty valuable lessons today.

Perpetuating the Inevitable
Wed, 15 Jun 2005

I fucked up big today. I did something I said I wouldn't do... I cheated on my guy with Mr. Pretty. I'm such a fucking dork! I know why I did it, not that I'm trying to excuse my behavior, but understanding the "why" of it may help me to not do it again.

Let's start with last night... My guy told me that he's falling in love with me. That's sweet except for the fact that I'm terrified of commitment. Fuck, I thought I was making progress with this. Dammit! I guess it can be said that I'm making some progress based on the fact that I feel like shit for cheating.

So here I sit while my guy in the other room with no idea what the hell I've done. What I do know for certain is that I will not tell him - it may serve to alleviate my own guilt but it will do nothing for him. I'll keep this bit of information to myself then try like hell to figure out where my head is.

Sex, swingers, and orgies, oh my!

Thu, 05 Jan 2006

Last week, in a moment of sex addict weakness, I joined one of those adult web sites that hook you up with singles in your area. It was such a bad idea! Now I have access to all the like-minded, sex-crazed freaks that live near me.

I checked my account tonight and had 20 messages from men who want to have sex with me. I responded to one guy who is coming to town at the end of January and wants to get together for a night. I know I shouldn't have, but I'm weak. And he's really hot. I should have hit the "delete my account" button, but I didn't. Dammit! I guess I still have the option to NOT meet the guy, right? I don't mind being freaky in bed, I just can't get freaky in bed with everyone I meet.

Since I broke things off with the boyfriend, I've been struggling quite a bit with my addiction. I've slept with two of my fuck-buddies, but did decline two separate invitations to "private" parties for New Year's Eve. I woke the next morning feeling pretty good about my decision.

I'm definitely better off now than I was a year ago, so that's good. I'll just keep working hard at keeping my clothes on and my legs closed.

By the way...
Sun, 08 Jan 2006
I'm so freakin' horny tonight, I could just cry!!

My convictions... or lack thereof.
Sun, 15 Jan 2006
Yesterday I saw the ex-BF. I had almost forgotten how much I loved him and how much I miss him until he showed up on my doorstep. He said he needed to pick up some paperwork he left here, but I know that was only half the reason. He was also horny. I don't think he walks around trying to be sexy, but he *is* fucking sexy as hell. Asshole.

I know I shouldn't have, but I let him kiss me with those beautiful full, soft lips. Damn. He held me and we kissed; I've always felt so safe in his arms. He is a huge guy; not fat at all. Hell, his biceps are the size of my thighs. His chest is massive. Fucking asshole! Doesn't he realize I have a hard time saying no to him. Argh.

Anyway, I did say no. I told him that the one thing he really taught me while we were together is that I need to stay true to my convictions. We aren't in a committed relationship, or even dating for that matter, so I didn't think it was right to have sex with him. I told him that I was done with meaningless sex. He looked a little hurt and said, "but it's not meaningless at all when we're together." Sweet sentiment, but no. He held me a while longer and told me how much he misses me. "Are you sure you just don't miss the sex?" I said. "No. I miss *you* and your sense of humor and your intelligence." Aw. Fucker.

After talking a while, I agreed to meet him later for a couple of drinks. We sat around and talked and watched a movie. One drink later and we've got our clothes off. Fuck me. Yeah, I said it. Fuck me. Dammit, I just couldn't help myself. It was just so comfortable being there with him. I miss that feeling. I realize that I miss the closeness and not so much the sexual act.

Yeah, I still get horny, but I'd rather live a lifetime with that closeness than a lifetime of meaningless sex. Right now, I can say that I don't want to have sex with him again. I'm not sure what tomorrow will bring, but I'll just continue to take it one day at a time, hoping that I'll make the right decision then.

I should charge for my services...
Fri, 20 Jan 2006

...except that would make me a prostitute. Damn labels anyways!

Here I go again, trying to justify having sex with strangers while trying to keep control of my sexual addiction. Dammit. Is it so wrong to have sex with someone because there's chemistry and a mutual attraction? I'm a full-grown adult. Shouldn't I have the freedom to make those choices without feeling like I'm losing the battle? Maybe I'm just not clear in my definition of sex addict versus consensual sex between willing partners.

My problem is that I love sex. I love the feeling and the endorphins and being wanted and making my partner feel that ecstasy. What's so wrong with that? And what about my Christian views? I keep fighting myself on this because I'm confused about what is right and what is wrong about having sex with someone just because it feels good. I'm protected. We're both adults. What the hell? I'm a recovering Catholic, but still hold a lot of views the church slammed into my head as a child. Will I go to hell for what I do? Oi!

All I know is that I don't want to get back to that place I was last year when I felt that sex was all I had. Sex was how I defined myself then. I don't see myself as the same person today. I've grown tremendously in the last year and I want to be careful not to get back to the hell I was in before. But, I just love sex.

Dammit, I hate these fights I have with myself. I guess as long as I'm not hurting myself or someone else in the process then I should be able to do what I want. Or not. Hell.

Thinkin` about being naughty
Fri, 07 Apr 2006
Horny I am. Horny I'll be. Unless...

...unless I hit the swingers club tonight. I'm sure to get laid; sure to have some fun without any limitations or commitment. What I'm feeling is a sense of loss for the "good ol' days" when fucking for fun was, well, fun.

Somehow, fucking for fun turned into a lot of pain and feelings of worthlessness. Am I over that now? I don't know, but it feels like I am. Maybe that's because I haven't been to the club in quite some time. Maybe it's because I haven't seen any of my fuck buddies in awhile because I've needed to get my head on straight.

All I really know is that I'm feeling frisky and want to have some free-wheeling fun.

Okay, honesty time. I'm actually a little pissed right now and want to just say "fuck it." If I take my own advice though, I'd know that anytime you have to say "fuck it," it's probably not a good choice.

What to do? What to do? I could stay home and get some rest. I could hook up with my friend Kitty and go to the bar. I could go to the club. Hm. Right now, I'm not sure what I'll do, but I'll make sure to give a full report tomorrow.

You gotta love them swingers!

Sat, 08 Apr 2006

Well, as you can assume by the title, I did go to the swingers club last night. My friend, Kitty, went with me. She had never been before and was pretty nervous. I was nervous because I wasn't sure I wanted Kitty to see me naked - we're friends, but you gotta draw the line somewhere.

Within two minutes of entering the club, we were approached by several ~~men~~ creepy dudes looking for a hookup. We weren't interested in what they had to offer and told them we were lesbian. I know, that statement would usually lead to the next, inevitable question, "can I watch?" In the swingers club, however, that statement means "No, I'm not sucking your dick. Now move along." And they did.

About a minute later, we were approached by a nice looking 30-something who wanted us to watch him masturbate. Cool. We followed him to a room and awkwardly stood there wondering

91

how much of ourselves to reveal to the other. See, I can cum just watching a guy please himself, but if I'm hesitant to get naked in front of Kitty, do I really want her to hear me orgasm? See my dilemma? Anyway, we watched as this guy did his thing and we both let him touch and lick our breasts. I was pretty fucking turned on but held back because of Kitty. Funny thing though, when we talked about it later, we both said we wanted to do more but were unsure if we should. I guess we know now.

We went back out into the main room, sat down, and were again immediately approached by several men. One guy asked Kitty if she wanted to do a threesome with him and his girlfriend. That would have been fine except that the dude was old enough to be her grandpa. Just weird. She turned him down. The next guy to approach her was a bit creepy too. He was too old, had a fucked up grill and spoke in very broken English. Kat kicked me so I put my arm around her and acted like I was nuzzling her neck. He took the hint and left. In the meantime, I was talking with a nice looking black man with very nice hands. We chatted a few minutes and when I saw a nice guy with Kitty, me and my guy decided it was safe, so we found a room for a hook up.

I wanted to do the fishbowl, but he was a bit shy about it, so we opted for a room with a semi-sheer curtain. We played a bit, he got a great blow job, then the real fun began. All I can say is this guy definitely knows how to eat pussy! Hell yeah! *I'm having a hard time typing right now... ah, the memories* Whew. Anyway, we fucked like animals, caught our breath, then got dressed and went back out into the main room.

Kitty had gone off with her guy so me and my guy sat and talked until she came back. We both smiled at each other, knowingly, and couldn't wait to leave so we could dish. I told Kitty about my guys extraordinary skill and she told me about her guys extra small penis. Apparently, he made up for it with his extraordinary skill. So, we were both happy.

So, at the end of the day, we both had a great time. Kitty had her first swingers' club experience and I got to remember how much I love the place AND got laid.

Overall, a good time was had by all.

Chapter Six:
Craving Love

Having a real relationship while struggling with a sexual addiction and fighting the effects of sexual abuse, is somewhere near impossible. It's not that I haven't wanted a real relationship with a good man, but because of the issues I was dealing with, I kept choosing all the wrong men. They were either alcoholic, "recovering" drug addicts, players, or a combination of all three. I had this insane ability to pick out the guy who looked, acted, and seemed normal, but was the absolute opposite of normal. That guy was familiar and comfortable to me, even though he was dealing with his issues, too. It certainly wasn't good for me, but fit me like my favorite fuzzy sweater.

Now, I'm pretty good at picking up on the signs of crazy. At the first sign of any red flags, I run for the hills. I no longer try to help him heal his wounds or become the good man I see underneath the rough exterior; he has to do that on his own...

The boy who saved me

Thu, 05 Aug 2004

I think I was the most confused when I was a teenager. Not only was I experiencing all the angst that a "normal" teen would, but I was also on an emotional rollercoaster due to the sexual abuse. Each day brought a new emotion but one thing was consistent, I wanted to die.

Thank God I met Don. We went to the same junior high and high school and the second I saw him, I fell in love. He had blonde hair and a beautiful smile. He was shorter than me but it didn't make a difference, I saw something in him that melted my heart.

Me and Don hung around most of the same people so we were usually going to the same parties, etc. He was on the football team and I was a pompon girl. We always had a thing for each other but we never really hooked up. We did kiss once on my 13th birthday during a round of spin the bottle and it was fantastic.

Don and I would talk for hours on the phone. We talked about everything and nothing at all. Once when I was away camping with my family, he wrote a letter that was waiting for me when I got home. It was the sweetest letter I've ever received and I still have it today.

What Don doesn't realize is that he saved my life, many times. I remember him "talking me down" (literally and figuratively) during many of my suicidal times. He never ran or thought I was crazy. For some reason, he stayed and talked and helped me through whatever it was I was going through at the time. Once we were sitting atop the monkey bars at a park. This sounds stupid now, but I wanted to jump. I know we were only high enough for me to break a leg or something, but I was crying for help and he heard me. He sat there with me for more than two hours and rubbed my hair and reassured me that everything would be okay. That was only one of the many times he made me believe there was a reason to live. I don't know if I could ever thank him enough for what he did for me.

Don married a girl from high school and has two children. I think he's happy. I hope he is. He deserves the best of everything for being one of the best human beings I have ever met.

Scissors and Hershey Kisses
Tue, 10 Aug 2004
Why can't you just love me?
The longer I wait the worse I feel
I know that love isn't supposed to hurt
But this does
Maybe it's not really love at all

Maybe I'm just afraid of not having anyone;
Of dying alone
Maybe I am not worthy of love at all
Maybe you're not the right one

Am I an idiot for not seeing it?
Or are you the asshole for letting it go on
Can't you see that I hurt
Every time you call me your "friend"

What the fuck does that mean anyway?
You want to spend the rest of your life
with someone you only call a friend?
You are an idiot, as am I
I know I need to end this thing we have
Whatever the hell it is
I can't seem to get any real explanation from you
All I hear is "time"

You say you want to grow old with me
Is that because you're afraid of dying alone
And I'm the best thing that's come along so far?
They say everyone can be replaced

It just hurts so much
Because I know I wouldn't be where I am without you
Is our time together done?
Have we learned everything we can?

Fuck, I hate this shit
The broken heart and not knowing how to go on
The reality that you don't really want me after all
Maybe no one ever will.

Tonight, I cried.
Sat, 14 Aug 2004
What a night I've had. I had this great chat with this great
guy who really helped me see myself and to get a different

perspective on some things. He even made me cry... in a good way.

I have to admit that I am scared as hell that I'll never find that guy who will love me for me, warts and all, and that I'll die old and alone. I'm like everyone else, I want a lasting relationship with someone who thinks I'm the most beautiful person in the world; who laughs at my weird sense of humor (and actually gets it); who believes in me and supports me. I would absolutely do the same for him, without question.

I want to be open enough to "see" that person if he comes my way, but will I be? I'm not expecting a miracle, just a nice guy who doesn't beat me or want to rape my kids, who isn't an alcoholic or drug addict, and who can hold a job for an extended period of time. He needs to be comfortable in his own skin. (Oh, and he has to be great in bed or willing to learn.) Is there anybody out there?

I'm in a relationship right now, if that's what this thing is called, but he lives 1,000 miles away. He's a great guy who has taught me a lot but I think our time is done. I love him so much, but I don't think he feels the same. That's hard for me to admit, but I have to be honest with myself or I will forever be stuck where I am right now. I wish he loved me like I love him, but he doesn't. At least he never says so. I know he "cares for me" but shit, I "care for" my fucking dogs. I need more than that. I don't know. It makes me so sad and I feel so pathetic. What the fuck is so wrong with me that no one can love me? What the fuck am I doing wrong? Man!

My new friend told me tonight that since I've already been through so much in my life, I can get through this. I know that's true, I'm just sad and scared. I will survive this just as I've survived everything fucking thing else in my fucking stupid ass shit hole life. FUCK FUCK FUCK FUCK FUCK!!!!! Apparently I have some more work to do. I have to love myself first. Argh! This is such hard work and I'm so tired.

"If pussy presents itself, I`m going to take it....."
Tue, 17 Aug 2004

That's what my guy "friend" said to me one evening right after he insisted that my pussy was his alone. He doesn't want me sharing my pussy with anyone else. But, as far as he goes, "if pussy presents itself, I'm going to take it." Nice.

I don't know what's worse, him being honest about his extracurricular activities and having a different set of rules for me, or me saying that I would be faithful while my brain is saying, "fuck that."

I've been fighting with myself the last couple of weeks because I want him to read my online journal but at the same time, I don't. He needs to read it so he knows who I am and what struggles I face every day. At the same time, I know that if he does read it, he won't want to be with me anymore. At least that's what I think, based on our previous conversations.

I'm just tired of not being completely honest with him. I've said before that I love him but if I can't share this stuff with him, how good is our relationship? He sees me as strong, positive, intelligent, and able to face anything. I'm afraid for him to see the "real" me... the scared girl who has sex to relieve stress, who feels worthless, and who struggles everyday with depression. I'm afraid to disappoint him because I hold him in such high regard.

I truly wouldn't be where I am today without his support. He believes that I can do anything and he encourages me to try. He really is a wonderful person and I don't want to lie to him anymore. I'm so scared of losing him forever but I can't continue lying to myself either. I just don't know what to do.

Just another day in paradise
Fri, 10 Sep 2004
Life has been a little ho hum for me lately; a little sad. Like the title says, "just another day in paradise." I'm not complaining, just stating a fact. I realize that some days are going to be worse than others and some are going to better. I'm still of the mindset that says "the glass if half full" so I'm okay.

I talked to my boyfriend about our relationship and it actually went pretty well. I'm still not sure where we are headed but I have a better idea as to where we are now. I'm still working on believing that I deserve a good man in my life. I'm not sure he is the one that I need but he is what I have right now. The relationship is serving its purpose and I'll just have to go with that for the moment.

I do love him very much and I'm fighting my sexual addiction everyday in order to honor our relationship. That's what I need to do to keep things sane in my head. I'm having a tough time of it today. I just want to head out to a club tonight and pick up some random guy and fuck the shit out of him. I won't, but I want to. I hate fighting with myself like this, but I know I'm a step ahead each time I don't give in.

I guess the other thing that's bugging me is the fact that every one of my girlfriends has a fucking boyfriend right now. I'm happy for them but jealous at the same time. I want a guy who's devoted and chasing my ass around... I guess I just want my guy to be in town. Argh! I know it sounds stupid and childish but it is how I feel right now.

I have a lot on my mind so I haven't been sleeping very well. I guess that's all I have for now.

Peace.

Okay, now this is the truth
Sun, 12 Sep 2004

My problem is my loneliness. I am so profoundly lonely and I just can't shake it. I know that it's my problem and that I need to fix it myself, I just hate the feeling.

The emptiness I feel is so deep, like the Grand Canyon. There have been so many changes in my life in the last couple of months and I'm trying to work through them. The hardest part for me is losing my friends who helped to fill some of the void I feel. I know that's not the reason to have friends and, in a way, I was using them but without bad intentions. I have just lost so much lately and it's really starting to affect me, especially with the realization that I've also lost my friends.

Yes, I am disappointed in the ones who lose themselves in their guy. It's as if they suddenly can't decide what to have for dinner or which team they like. They defer everything to the guy and end up losing themselves completely. Have a fucking opinion and some independent thought! I guess maybe I was helping to fill some of their void while they were waiting for Mr. Wonderful to come along.

I'm also disappointed in myself. I feel kind of selfish for being jealous of my friends, like I'm some sort of sad puppy sitting in the corner crying about this and that when I should be helping myself. I am all alone in this world and have only myself to depend on, but fuck that's a lonely feeling. Am I supposed to feel as if I can't count on anyone but myself? Or am I just throwing an adult-sized tantrum? I like to believe that I am here whenever someone needs me but maybe that's just an inflated ego. Fuck, I don't even know anymore.

I just hate feeling as if I have no one. No one. No one. No one. No one. No one. No one. That's exactly how I feel. I want to be able to cry on someone's shoulder and have them NOT turn it around so suddenly we are talking about them. I want to be in a solid and committed relationship instead of this shit I'm actually in, fooling myself into believing that he loves me! Ha! If you love me, just fucking say it! Don't make me guess! I'm just hanging on to your words and trying to imagine that you love me. You say you want a strong woman in your life, how about a REAL woman? You know, one who has FEELINGS and is allowed to express them without fear that you're going to break her heart because she's not strong enough for you. Fuck! Why can't I just feel? What the fuck is so wrong with that? You call it strength but it actually means that I'm not allowed to feel anything except strong and positive and fucking shoot me in the fucking head right now cause I can't take this shit anymore! AARRGGHHHHHHH!

I just want to cry and scream so much right now. But no! I can't cry. I have to be strong for EVERYONE else in this fucking world and forget that I have feelings. I'm apparently not allowed.

I am so afraid. I'm scared that I'm going to be alone for the rest of my life. I don't want to die alone. I think that would be the worst thing ever. Die alone bitch, no one wants you or has time for you. Ha ha! Die alone! Fuck!

Listening

Sat, 18 Sep 2004

I've been thinking a lot about words and what they actually mean. We mostly go around talking but never really take the time to understand what it is we're really saying.

I talked to my guy a couple of days ago and he was very upset about the email I sent him. It got me to thinking a lot about the words we use. I complain that he calls me "friend" even after we've been seeing each other for almost a year and a half. I finally realized he has told me the truth all along but I didn't hear the words. Friend means friend, nothing more. I wanted to hear words that just weren't there. When he said "I care for you," that's exactly what he meant; he cares for, NOT loves, me. We are friends and he cares for me. That's it. So I've been crying because I wanted more than that but it's my own fault for not really listening.

It's funny because I always tell others that God gave us two ears and one mouth so we should listen twice as much as we talk. I think maybe I should use that advice myself. A dear friend told me of a quote she heard which says, "I don't take the advice I give because I'm not the type of people I'd give advice to."

Romance and freaks

Sun, 03 Oct 2004

So I went on my first date since my break up with G. The guy is very nice, romantic, intelligent, and talks a lot! I'm not sure if he really talks a lot or if I was losing interest because I really needed a cigarette!

The date started out at Starbucks for coffee. Of course, going out for coffee first gives you the opportunity (if the guy is a freak) to finish the cup and say, "it was nice meeting you" then leave as fast as you can. We had a nice time, talked about relationships, kids, work, etc. then decided to have dinner because the date was going so well.

Dinner started out nice, we talked some more, ordered steak, talked more, held hands. Okay, I have to interrupt myself to say that I just realized I definitely lost concentration because of the nicotine issue. Crap man! Cigarettes are bad, bad, bad! I actually lost interest in a perfectly nice guy because I needed a fix! Wow. Anyway, we had a nice dinner and dessert, found out that we have a lot in common, walked outside and talked some more. We said our goodbyes with a hug then I got in my car and left. Of course I lit up immediately.

Since I got home I've been wondering about the date. We've established that I needed a fix but I think it also may be too soon after G. Maybe I'm scared of finding a normal guy who isn't an alcoholic or drug addict and who actually wants a commitment. Maybe there's something wrong with new guy and that's why I feel weird. I don't know.

Okay, so I'll go on another date with the new guy and bring my smokes this time.

And ANOTHER thing...

Wed, 29 Dec 2004

Tonight, I had a very in-depth conversation with my friend Guido. We were talking about being in love and what it could be that's stopping me from finding Mr. Wonderful. I think I figured it out.... I don't trust a man with my heart and my soul. They've been so damaged over the years that I'm finding it difficult to ever imagine spending the rest of my life with someone who could easily take my vulnerabilities and angrily wave them in front of me when the mood suited him.

I remember an incident when I was married... my husband was drunk and decided to pick a fight. I'd been married to the man long enough to know that you don't even try to discuss anything worthwhile when he's in that state, but he was drunk and didn't give a thought to it. He started out by telling me that I was just too fucked up for him, that he also had a bad childhood, and that it didn't affect him at all. Right. Anyway, he then told me that I probably wasn't even molested as a child - that I made it up - but even if I was molested that I must have enjoyed it. How fucked up is that?

I took eleven years of that shit from him. Okay, it was more like seven, but damaging nonetheless. I know, I should have divorced him much sooner, but I was trying to keep the family together. I commented to Guido tonight that I truly felt that if I had cancer and lost a breast, he would have left me. His own selfishness would have come before helping to take care of and love the person he committed himself to in his vows. When I took my vows, I took them seriously... for better or worse, in sickness and in health. I meant the words I spoke, but he didn't. I would have supported him 100% if he chose to get treatment for his alcoholism, but he wanted to drink more than he wanted his family. He didn't take his vows seriously at all.

I guess I'm just looking for a man who would treat me as well as I would treat him. Someone who would stand by me when things got rough, and who would let me stand by him in the same manner. I would NEVER take his vulnerabilities and use it against him just because I was angry. NEVER! I'm not looking for someone to take care of me, I'm looking for someone who appreciates me and loves me just the way I am. I would do the same for him.

Breaking my spirit
Thu, 10 Feb 2005

There was a year in my life that I like to call "hell." I was 17 and made the "grown-up" decision to get married to a guy I knew for about six months. I was in that rebellious stage and determined to marry the man I loved. My mom, being so much wiser than my 17 years, decided to sign the consent form with full understanding and knowledge that I may need a place to come back to if things didn't work out. I was ecstatic.

My new husband, David (not his real name), was kind, considerate, compassionate, and caring. For about a week. After that, it was just like hell.

The breaking of my spirit started with name calling and progressed to slapping and punching for anything David conceived as a slight. I wasn't "allowed" to leave the house without permission and had a strict time limit when I did. I couldn't see my family or friends because he thought they were a bad influence on me. David controlled what I ate, what I drank, when I slept, everything. His behavior was so erratic and unstable that I never knew what to expect. We owned 13 weapons and had a reloading station at our home. It was my job to reload the shells for each round of target practice. Every time I loaded one, I secretly wondered if it would be the one he used to kill me with. Needless to say, I was terrified and knew I had to find a way to escape.

I was afraid to tell anyone what was going on for fear of another beating, or worse, that he'd kill me or one of my family members. My mom tried to keep in touch but, as I found out years later, was often told that I didn't want to talk to her. Of course, she knew something was terribly wrong but didn't have access to me and didn't know what to do.

Everything came to an end one day when I was home sick. I had a high fever, chills, a cough, and didn't feel well at all. David returned from work and immediately started pinching and poking at me. I repeatedly asked him to stop, but he continued on. I'd had enough. Without even thinking, I sprang off the couch, put him in a head-lock, threw him down, and started beating the living shit out of him. I punched him over and over and over again, until I was sure he got the message. "I'm sick. Leave me alone you stupid, worthless, fucking waste of skin!" Argh! Apparently he got the message; we filed for divorce about two weeks later. Oh, and he never even tried to hit me again.

People look at me now, seeing a confident and strong woman, and wonder how I could have stayed with an abusive husband. What a lot of people don't understand is that the breaking of your spirit happens slowly. He slaps you then apologizes profusely, and you *want* to believe it was a one-time thing, so you forgive him. Unfortunately, the cycle repeats itself and continues on before you even know what's happening. Suddenly, you feel scared, defeated and helpless to do anything about your situation. Taking that step out is the hardest part of all, but so well worth it in the long run.

At the age of 18, I was divorced. It took me months to feel comfortable enough to not look over my shoulder constantly. David moved on right away and found a new girlfriend at work. I don't know what's happened to him since and I don't care. I'm just glad he's out of my life.

Little step back, little step forward, little step...
Sun, 24 Apr 2005

On Friday night I met, T… he's a nice guy. I've spent most of the weekend with him and no, not like you would imagine. Actually, we've spent a lot of time just talking about our pasts and what we want in the future. He's been very honest about his background, his mistakes, his past relationships, and what he's been doing to change it. I've been honest about my sexual abuse issues, my sexual addiction, my past relationships, my fear of commitment, and what I'm doing to change it. So far, neither of has run away from the other. I guess it takes one pained soul to truly understand the other.

I was actually *nervous* before going to meet him on Saturday night. That's not like me at all! I want, so much, to do it right this time. I don't want another fuck buddy out of the deal - I want a real relationship. I could have let him come home with me, but I didn't! I had the house to myself and I didn't invite him in.

Believe me, I wanted to, but I can't expect things to change if I don't change them for myself.

Today, we went to the lake and just talked and held each other. It was awesome. I don't know where this will lead, but whatever the outcome, I've learned a few more things about myself, and those lessons are invaluable.

You know things are going badly when...

Sat, 21 May 2005

You know things are going badly when... every relationship you end up in is with someone who's either an alcoholic, a drug addict, or a womanizer. And that does seem to describe every long-term relationship I've ever been in.

The Devil (aka my first husband) / Alcoholic. Womanizer. Hitter: I met him about a week after I broke up with my high school boyfriend. D blew in on a motorcycle, looking all cool n' shit, talking sweet, and gave me his undivided attention. When he said he'd pick me up at 7:00 p.m., he was there on time and usually carrying flowers or some such girly thing. I fell in love quickly and was barely 17 years old when we married. A week after the wedding is when the hitting started, along with his self-esteem-shattering name calling. There I was, all 5'7" 130 lbs of me being called fat, ugly and stupid then smacked in the face just because he felt like it. D was an alcoholic and a womanizer. The marriage ended a year later. That was the day I beat the fuck out of him, you know, the day I wasn't going to take his shit anymore. I guess once he realized I could kick his ass my usefulness wore off.

Mr. Machismo / Alcoholic. Womanizer: I met M about six months after I divorced the Devil. He was 12 years older than me, 6' tall, blonde hair, blue eyes, and one hella Swedish fucking hottie! M taught me a lot about sex. I'm not really sure what else we had in common, but we both certainly liked experimenting sexually. He liked it so much that he "shared the wealth" with many other women. Ain't that sweet? We were together about a year and a half, then just sort of quit seeing each other. No real drama, no goodbyes, just "hm... I haven't seen M in a while... wonder what he's up to."

The Biker / Alcoholic: I met B one night while playing pool in my local bar. We were on our second or third game when I couldn't quite reach the shot (plus I wanted to really get his attention) so I climbed on the pool table and made my shot while ass-up on all fours. B was really a sweet guy who carried around a rough exterior. The only problem in our relationship was his drinking. He didn't get violent or anything, he held a good job, and was very kind to me, but he was always drunk. In fact, he's the one who helped me discover my love of tequila. Our relationship ended early one morning after B left for work. His roommate decided to come into our room and rape me. Obviously, things just weren't the same after that.

The Daddy (aka my second husband) / Alcoholic. Hitter: I met D while hanging out with a local metal band. He was a friend of the bass guitarist and I was fucking the drummer. Jump forward a year and a half and there we are at a barn party, talking and laughing when and I asked him out. We dated seven months before we got hitched. We were married for 11 years and had two kids. The first four years were fine. After our first daughter was born, everything went to hell and quick. D decided it was okay to get drunk and punch or choke me, he often referred to his mom as a whore, and generally had no respect for women. I blame myself for a lot of this fiasco because the warning signs were there, I just refused to see them. I'm not sorry, because I did get two wonderful kids out of it, but it was pure hell. The hitting stopped on my 30th birthday when he tried to choke me and I threw the asshole into a head-lock and beat the fuck out of him. Again, another victim of my pent-up rage.

The Golf Pro / Alcoholic. Womanizer: I met M one night, made out with him in his truck, fucked his brains out for two weeks, then he dumped me. I was heart-broken. A week later, he called and said he couldn't live without me. So there began our one and a half year freak/fuck-fest. M was 14 years older than me and really knew what he was doing in bed. With him, it was the first time in years that I actually felt like a woman. I wasn't someone's wife or mother, I was a desirable woman and he let me know it. Unfortunately, he was fucking everything in town, as I found out later. Apparently, it got so bad that a woman's husband poisoned M's dog because of his affair with her.

The Red Neck / Alcoholic. Womanizer: I met J one night, purposely gave him the wrong address and talked to him on the phone while he drove around looking for my house. I told him about the red teddy I was wearing, how my legs were spread and my pussy was ready for some dick. I thought it was funny. He didn't. Six months later I ran into him again, gave him the right address this time, and that started our year and a half long relationship. With J, it felt as if I were raising another child. I know that his energy and outlook on life is part of what appealed to me, but there are times when you have to be serious and take responsibility for your life. He just didn't want any part of that. J had a very rough up-brining and dealt with the scars of that by drinking heavily. Our relationship was pretty stormy and ended when he started fucking his cousin. Yep, his cousin.

The African Prince / Alcoholic. Womanizer: I met G while he was visiting my neighbor. We didn't get together until six months later and I fell madly and deeply in love. I know he "cared" for me and he even said "I love you" once, but I also know that he's not capable of being with just one woman. He's an alcoholic, smokes a great deal of weed, and sleeps with quite a few women (one in each port?). That ended when I admitted my sexual addiction to him. I guess what's good for the goose really isn't good for the gander.

From what I can garner, I seem to be attracted to any man who is an alcoholic and has issues with intimacy and commitment. As I've said before, "my picker is broke." I wonder what it is about the alcoholic that seems to draw me to them? Is it their own wounded spirit and my co-dependency? Was I a raging alcoholic in a past life and now I'm paying for my sins? All I know is that I can't go anywhere near an AA meeting or all hell will let loose.

Is that love staring me in the face or are you just happy to see me?

Sat, 02 Jul 2005

Somewhere, around the age of three, when bio-dad was fondling and fucking me, all-the-while saying things like "I love you," my emotional brain got all screwed up thinking that what he was doing to me equaled love. For so long, I was taught that sex equals love.

Rewiring my own thinking has been difficult. As an adult, logic tells me that love is love and great sex with love is just a bonus. Emotionally believing it has been a whole other issue for me. Yes, sex is a very important part of a love relationship, but it's not everything. I used to fall in love after having incredible sex thinking that was normal and I would just as easily <u>not</u> love someone because the sex was just "so-so." Now I'm in a relationship that is full of love and it's hard for me to recognize the good stuff coming from it; my mind keeps going back to "sex equals love." I'm having a particularly hard time because I have no interest in sex at the moment due to an increase in the number of flashbacks and nightmares I'm having.

I guess I'm really having a hard time defining myself as something other than a sex addict. Sex was my drug of choice, temporarily enabling me to forget the pain inside with a rush of endorphins and fake feelings. Now I'm dealing with the pain, dealing with the memories, and dealing with love - all at the same fucking time! What's really happening is that I'm not sure if I truly know the feel, smell, and taste of love.

I'll just continue on with my counseling, journaling, and self-analysis in hopes I figure this out relatively soon, hopefully sometime before I fucking die. Geesh!

Fuck Romance

Sun, 23 Oct 2005

Fuck romance
and soppy chick flicks
that make us believe
all is possible
and love is true

Fuck those sweet little commercials
where boy sees girl
girl sees boy
and magic happens in an instant

It ain't fucking reality girls!
Reality is your man farting when he sleeps
and forgetting to put the toilet seat down
in the morning

Reality is your man not understanding
a fucking thing you say, like you're
speaking a foreign language and
your jaw is wired shut

Reality is fights over money and child-rearing
and religion and sex...
he wants to spend on whatever HE wants, he doesn't
do diapers, God is a farce, and he wants sex
whenever he wants sex, regardless of what you want

Reality is your man forgetting your birthday,
your anniversary, and Christmas
then saying to you, "it's just another day."

Fuck the players who tell you want you NEED to hear
then crushing your heart with one action or word
without a thought as to what it does to you

Fuck us gullible women who've been brainwashed
into believing romance actually exists
and that the man of our dreams will
rescue us from our hidden dungeons in hell

Fuck the corporate structures
who continue perpetuating this farce
while selling us glimmers of hope

Fuck romance! It doesn't exist.

Affirmations
Tue, 21 Feb 2006
Each morning I wake, ready to face the day
Each morning you wake saying, "how can I fuck with her?"
I try my hardest to ignore you, but you're hard not to see,
Jumping up and down and waving your arms

I've tried so hard to be nice or deny you're there
But you won't let it go
What the hell do I have to do to make you go away?

You dirty piece of shit...
Stop talking to me like that!
Ugly, fat, no one wants you, failure...
Now I understand why people shoot themselves in the head

That's it, motherfucker! You've said all you're gonna say
I will not stand for your crap anymore!
I know I'm better than that and I'm certainly better than you
You're the one who is a fuck up and a failure
You're the one who's trying to tear me down, and why?
Just because you think you can and you've been so good at it
before?
Well, "fuck you Mr. Conscious!"
Today is a new day

I will not let the tapes of the past invade my head any longer
I will not let bio-dad's actions define me
I will not let you have any more of my soul

I will win
I will succeed
I am beautiful
I am an intelligent woman
I am lovable

You, my dear, are gone...

Chapter Seven:
Becoming a Survivor

We shall draw from the heart of suffering itself
the means of inspiration and survival.
Sir Winston Churchill

A new perspective.....

Sat, 16 Oct 2004

I received a very thoughtful private message from a friend
and this is what he said...

*"The purpose of life is to recreate yourself anew in each moment,
in the next grandest version of the greatest vision ever you held about
Who You Are".*

*In other words, I don't know you well at all, but I'd venture to
say that the grandest vision you hold of yourself is not SEX ADDICT.*

*I have had issues and challenges with sex addiction myself, but I
will never identify myself as a sex addict. Not because I'm in denial --
quite the contrary -- but because I believe the identification of oneself
of a particular thing is what keeps that particular thing going and
growing.*

It keeps it alive.

Imagine if you decided, right now, to label yourself as a wonderful, smart, loving, sensitive, kind woman who has issues with sex addiction. I believe that much about you and I've only been exchanging emails with you for the past week.

Imagine adopting these beliefs in your life:

I am not an addict.

I am not worthless.

I am not shameful.

I want to sincerely thank the friend who wrote me this -- it was what I needed to hear. I hadn't even thought about the labels I was placing on myself and how they could affect me. I alone have the option and control to "re-label" myself so I can continue to move forward in a healthy way.

I am so many sorts and colors and shades of fucked up, I`m starting to find myself amusing.

Wed, 22 Dec 2004

I'm not entirely sure what's caused my recent bout of introspection, but I think it's been a good exercise for me. I've been trying to understand <u>exactly</u> what's going on in my head and I think I may have come to a conclusion... I feel "temporary." Temporary, as in, there's no permanency to my life - I don't feel solid or whole - like the other shoe is going to drop at any moment and I'll have to make another change. When I moved into my house six months ago, I thought it would help me find the peace I've been looking for. Funny thing is, I haven't even unpacked all my boxes yet.

It's fucking stupid that I let fear control so many aspects of my life. I know I have to take that first step, but I'm just so afraid to feel the extraordinary pain I've felt before.

I remember sitting in a group counseling session one evening, listening to the story of a woman there. The more she talked, the smaller I became. It's as if I could feel myself physically reducing in size to the point that I almost felt as if I were turning inside out. My head started to pound, my skin hurt, my heart felt as if it were going to stop. I don't know what it was about her story that made me feel that way, but I know that it was extremely painful and I'm afraid of feeling that again. Fear is stopping me from moving forward.

I'm afraid of what I'll remember. I'm afraid of what I've already forgotten. I'm afraid of feeling the emotional pain of reliving the experience. I'm afraid that I won't be able to control myself. I'm afraid I'll want to kill myself. I'm afraid of love. I'm afraid of not being loved. I'm afraid of life. I'm afraid of not living.

God, I really do want to heal and feel whole again. Can it ever be? I'm just dying inside and I don't know how to face the pain. God, please help me feel again. Please help me face my fear. Please help me.

Looking ahead
Thu, 23 Dec 2004
Well, I have decided to get some counseling. Yeah, I know, I should have decided that loooong ago, but there's no time like the present. It's weird because I don't necessarily feel depressed, but it's pretty obvious that I am. Choosing to relive that pain isn't

something that comes easy, but I have to do something to get over this hurdle. (Now that I think about it, the pain I'm in now isn't so fucking pleasant either. Hm.) I know it will be hard but I have to just face my fear and do it.

What's so fucked up is that I continue to say I'm a survivor, but I've been in the victim mode for a few months now. I guess I'm in my "two steps back" phase and need a nudge forward again.

I'm beginning to realize just how much the abuse has affected me in my adult life. My fear of commitment and involving myself in fucked up relationships is a result of the past, but I know I am the only one who can change that. I have to love me again and I have to feel worthy of love. I guess I'm just so angry that bio-dad took that away from me without a second thought. Now he's living his little life with his little wife in their little house and having a great fucking time! Asshole! How dare he do that to me or anyone else. My brother told me that the last time he talked to him, bio-dad went on and on about how he's a *minister* now and he doesn't have to repent for anything because he didn't do anything wrong. He had the fucking nerve to tell my brother that HE should repent for calling him Ben instead of dad. Right. What a fucking stupid-ass piece of shit he is! In fact, he should quit talking because he's breathing my air - stupid motherfucking waste of skin! Argh.

Anyway, yeah I'm angry, but it's only hurting me. I definitely need to work on that in counseling. I think I'll start working on a letter to bio-dad in order to get some of this shit out. I don't know that I'll send it, but maybe I'll post it for the world to see.... that may help me a little... I don't know. One step at a time.

A little game of hide and seek.

Thu, 13 Jan 2005

When you're hiding from yourself, where do you go? It's funny that I ask the question given I've been doing just that for many years. It's not the same as taking a road trip across the country, stopping in quaint little towns and soaking up the culture. Nor is it the same as flying to Maui, sitting on the beach and making friends with Roxanne, the local homeless woman who walks around town wearing May West gowns and hats and who has a live rooster in her shopping cart.

No, it's more like the things we fill our lives with in order to momentarily forget the negative thoughts rummaging through our heads, looking for a place to stay. Some people sleep, some eat, some use drugs and alcohol, some kick their dogs and beat their wife and kids, some binge and purge, some shop, some have meaningless sex. Pick your poison. Funny thing is, none of these habits or addictions really make us feel any better at all. They only serve to offer continued room and board to those negative thoughts we're so desperately trying to hide from.

Recognizing our hiding places and learning to cope with what we see is the hard part. I'd like to say I've done it myself, but I can't. How do you rewire years of self-doubt, mental abuse, emotional abuse, and sexual abuse in order to help the scared little girl with her arms raised who's ready to be picked up and held? People have said to me, "It's the past, let it go." Wow! Had I known it was so easy, well…

I am still learning to deal with my own demons, learning to find coping mechanisms, and learning to love myself in spite of those negative thoughts occupying my mind. It's been quite a journey full of tears, hair pulling, running, screaming, hating, and hitting, all done to myself because I couldn't take the pain – self-abuse at its best.

Yes, I'm still hiding, but the hiding places are becoming fewer as they are being replaced by positive thoughts and a change in attitude. Maybe someday I'll win this game of hide and seek and enjoy the multi-colored lollipop prize waiting for me at the finish line.

Normal is as normal does

Sat, 22 Jan 2005

So I'm sitting here alone on a Saturday night, bored out of my mind, wondering what the rest of the world is doing right now.

I imagine some of you are drinking yourselves into oblivion and hoping to get laid, some are on anxious first dates, while others are arguing with spouses or significant others. There are those contemplating suicide or binging and purging for the fourth time today. Some are stuffing their sorrows and pain with a half-gallon of ice cream and a bag of chips, while others are "exercising" their demons with another two hours at the gym. Like me, some of you are probably missing loved ones and best friends, just waiting for tomorrow to come so you can do it all over again.

When describing the human race, "normal" is not a word I use often. I don't think there is such a thing. We all have our dysfunction and issues to deal with and, depending on the scripts we were read as children, we have different ways of dealing with them. The key is finding a way to cope that isn't going to eventually kill us before we find the answers to our questions.

It's a tough world out there and we really only have ourselves to depend on. It would be nice to think the person you're standing next to would give their life for yours, but the chances are slim. Yeah, it sounds harsh, but, unfortunately, it's the reality of life. It doesn't mean they don't care, but remember, they're dealing with their own shit too. We humans are selfish.

So, here I sit, alone on a Saturday night, bored out of my mind, wondering what the rest of the world is doing right now.

Learning to fish

Thu, 24 Feb 2005

Give a man a fish and feed him for a day. **Teach** a man to fish and feed him for life.

-Chinese Proverb

This has been one of my favorite quotes of late. I use it quite frequently, whether talking with my kids, or talking to myself. For me, it's a great tool in becoming more centered, as opposed to self-centered. With the stress of everyday life hitting us in the face constantly, it's easy to become the center of our own universe. We should appreciate the lessons afforded us each day and pass them along with love and compassion, forgetting ourselves for a moment.

I know it's a rose-colored-glass dream, but it's all I have.

God bless.

I finally did it!

Wed, 09 Mar 2005

With some coaxing and prodding from a very dear friend, I finally made an appointment (for Friday) with a counselor. She actually specializes in trauma, so it should be good. Also, she's willing to accept a sliding fee since I don't currently have insurance.

I was reluctant to call before. Hell, I've had the number for a couple of months, but know that I need to act now before this shit gets any worse.

I've been fighting a lot with loneliness, grief, sadness, and loss. Add that to all of my abuse issues and you've got yourself one fucked up girl. But I'm on my way back, so watch out! Sound pretty confident, don't I?

So much...

Fri, 18 Mar 2005

It's been a strange week full of rollercoaster emotions. Counseling is going well. Granted, this is only the second week, but I haven't run away screaming yet, so it must be going pretty well. Funny thing is, we went through some of the crap that bio-dad did to me and others in my family and SHE even shook her head in disbelief. He is an evil man. She wants me to do some art therapy this week but I don't know if I can. For years now, I've continued to buy sketch pads, colored pencils, paint, you name it, but I haven't been able to pick them up and put my thoughts to paper. I'm scared, I guess. I know the stuff that's sitting just below the surface may come out and I'm afraid of what I'll see.

Ready to erupt

Tue, 22 Mar 2005

I'm just so incredibly sad today; have been for the past couple of days. I guess it's because I've experienced so many different types of loss lately... I no longer have a relationship with G, my oldest daughter moved to Utah, and my best friend is in love and devoting her time to her new man.

I'm not trying to cry and say "poor me," I'm just stating a fact. I'm sad and trying to deal with it. I don't have anyone I can turn to except myself, and I guess that IS the point in all this. I have to learn to emotionally stand on my own two feet. It sucks, let me just say that. I've basically stood on my own my entire adult life and my feet are tired as hell. They're sore and bleeding from all the standing I've done. I hate this so much.

What I'm really missing is human contact. I am so much inside myself and it's not the best place to be. I'm trying so hard to not replace one addiction with the other just because I'm lonely. I want to go out, have a few drinks, pick up some random guy and fuck all night. I want to eat everything I see until I'm huge as a house and no one will want me. I want to drive and drive and drive and never come back. I've even thought about prostitution. I mean, what the fuck? At least I'd be making some money. And hey, what about picking up a drug habit? That might be fun. Argh.

I've been in a semi-rage most of the day. The least little thing could set me off, so I just stayed to myself and warned those I love to stay away from me until this passes. I wrote this today to help ease my pain...

My skin. Hot to the touch. With a cool outer shell.
My appearance belies the truth.
There's a rage. Boiling. Just below the surface
Volcanic molten lava runs fiery through my veins
The anger, like carbon monoxide, sucking away my breath
I'm almost dead

So, I'm sitting here, trying to just let the feelings pass, lost inside my head, so incredibly sad.

The Random Thoughts in My Head
Wed, 23 Mar 2005
A tear shed alone
on a dusty desert highway
dried only by the sand
and the sun

But the pain
remains locked inside
the warrior with no shield

* * * * * *

No one hears me
my voice is silenced
by your preconceived notions
and your own guilt

I want to scream
out to the world
I HURT!

The pain
is crushing my lungs
and I can't breathe
but I remind myself
that's it's necessary for life

Can't you feel it?
Can't you hear it?
Can't you sense its presence?
It's wrapped around you
Screaming in your ear
You must be too busy to notice

I hate you

Forest Gump was right!
Thu, 24 Mar 2005

Life really is like a box of chocolates. Just look at those sampler boxes with all the different creme, nougat, coconut, and fruit filled morsels. Some of them I like, some of them I don't. You can be guaranteed that we don't all like the same things.

Life IS that sampler box when it's handing down problems. Some of the struggles are minor and go down easy while others take more time to digest. I was handed a nutty variety this time -

they don't taste so great, they're very hard to digest, and some of the nuts get stuck in your teeth, but you get through it.

I had so many losses recently and I needed time to be sad and grieve. I'll always love G because he is a good man, he's just not the man for me. Hopefully, when I'm feeling better about myself and get through some of this shit, God will send a good man my way. My daughter moved out of state, but she's happy and that makes me happy. She has the kindest soul of anyone I've ever known. I miss her terribly, but I'll see her over Mother's Day weekend. My best friend is in love with a great guy and truly happy for the first time since I've known her. I do miss her and her quirky sense of humor; I miss hanging out and coming up with new schemes to take over the world, but love has been good for her and I'm glad she is moving into the next phase of her life with a good man by her side.

Yes, I'm still grieving and I'm still sad, but I'm getting through. I guess this is part of standing on my own. I have to take what life gives me and just deal with it. I won't pretend that I like being by myself all the time, but it is what it is; maybe that's part of this life lesson. I just hope the lesson isn't that I'll be by myself forever, so "get used to it now, bitch."

So I'm trying to move on and get through this pain. I do know it will pass, but when you're right in the midst of it, it's hard to see anything hopeful on the other side. I guess it's a good thing I'm in counseling...

What the fuck?

Sat, 26 Mar 2005

I am so sick of hearing about little girls being abducted from their homes, being raped, and killed. I'm sick of hearing about entire families being killed by an estranged lover. I'm sick of hearing about children being left alone in the house, fending for themselves because their mom is too busy getting high to take care of them.

What the fuck is wrong with people? Why do these demons feel it's necessary to take out their adult problems on the children in their lives? YOU'RE A FUCKING ADULT! TAKE SOME RESPONSIBILITY!

I don't care if you were abused as a child. I don't care if your momma wouldn't give you jello for breakfast. I don't care if your daddy was in prison. Yes, as a child your life may have been difficult, but that gives you NO RIGHT to abuse the children you now have care of.

Guess what? I was HORRIBLY abused as a child and I would NEVER hurt another child the way I was. I LEARNED FROM MY ABUSE! Don't you remember how devastated you were when your grandpa fucked you with his shriveled old dick every night before bed? Don't you remember how long it took for the bruises to heal after your mom beat the shit out of you? Don't you remember how many times you hid the crack pipe from your dad because you couldn't endure another night of his insanity? Don't you remember?

Now put yourself in the place of your own child. Don't you think he's hurting just as bad now as you were then? Don't you think she'd rather have a hug and a kind word than hear you go on and on about how she'll never amount to anything? Don't you wish your own parent would have said those kind words to you? Think about your child.

Now that you remember, pick up the phone and call a counselor. Call a crisis hotline. Call someone and get some fucking help. It's not your child's fault that your parents treated you like shit! Quit taking it out on them. You have the ability to change your thinking. You have the ability to stop the cycle of abuse. It's up to you now.

Get some help.

Things to ponder

Sat, 02 Apr 2005

Yesterday's counseling was pretty rough. I want to heal but I'm just so reluctant to feel any more pain. We did some visualization work but all I could see was bloody hands. My breathing got very shallow, my body felt as if it were being crushed, and my head like it was going to explode. Needless to say, it wasn't the best thing in the world but gives me something to think about and work on. Mostly, I want to know where the bloody hands are coming from. Always more work to do.

I heard from my friend J last night, too. He wants me to go with him to another swinger's club. He's already been and said it was very exciting and very unlike the club we went to. It sounds like it could be a lot of fun, but I'm having so much trouble with the sex thing. What I mean is that I have trouble remembering why I am giving it up. What's so wrong with having sex with willing partners? I keep asking myself if it will really cause me emotional damage and if I'm just trying to justify my actions. I really do want to go, but keep telling myself I shouldn't.

Ack... I guess I'll figure it out and do the right thing. Anyone know what that is? Anyone? Anyone?

She's a rebel

Tue, 05 Apr 2005

I really don't know where my head is right now. The deeper I get into therapy, the harder this is for me. I'm rebelling, I guess. And I'm scared. I've lived for so long with the "me" I am now, that I feel as if I'm losing my identity. I don't know what sits on the other side and I'm so afraid.

I constantly ask myself who and what I'll be when this is done. Will I lose my sense of humor? Will I lose my compassion? Will anyone like me? Will I like myself? People keep telling me that the gains will certainly outweigh the losses, but I just don't see it yet.

I'm so consumed by pain, I can't see straight. The emotional pain of remembering and re-living what was done to me is enormous. I'm confused, I can't concentrate, and I'm making bad decisions because I don't know what to do. The physical pain is just as bad. It's as if I'm being squeezed around the middle so I have no air, I have horrific headaches that feel like a volcano ready to explode, and my body aches to the point that I don't want to move. I hurt.

I really do want to be confident and strong. I do. I'm just so fearful of what I'll become that I'm stifled in my work to regain my mental health.

I have to apologize, too, for not keeping up with everyone who reads my journal and whom I consider friends. I'm trying to sort this stuff out, but I'm finding that left to my own devices, I turn into a complete idiot. So please know that I think of you all daily and so appreciate all the support you continue to give me. Hopefully, I'll be back on track soon and then you won't be able to get rid of me, even if you try!

Minute by minute
Sat, 09 Apr 2005

Have you ever felt as if you had so much running through your head that you couldn't make a coherent thought? That's how I feel lately. If my head were a cheap motel, the sign out front would read "No Vacancy." There is no room at the inn. Lot full. No Parking. We have reached maximum capacity. You get the idea...

What I've been doing is living each day, minute by minute. It's all I can muster at the moment. In fact, it's to the point that I'm almost not functional in my daily life. I go to work and somehow meander through the day while looking busy. I come home and sit. I often think about sleep but don't get much. If I sleep, then I have to wake up and face the next day. So, I'm always exhausted. It's a vicious cycle.

Last week was the toughest yet. I've been acting out since my session the week prior. I know it's a rebellion, of sorts, but the knowledge of that doesn't stop me from being an idiot. I talked with my therapist about changing my treatment plan a bit so I am a little more functional day to day. Minute by minute. That's all I've got.

Bile

Mon, 06 Jun 2005

In my throat are the words I want to say

They rise like bile after a long night of tequila shooters

Stuck like a poorly-chewed piece of steak swallowed by a hungry man

Why do I hesitate to speak?

Maybe because I'm not comfortable with how the words sound

Maybe I'm just afraid to take the next step

Maybe I'm wrong

Maybe I'll chew a couple of Tums, chew on the words, and see if regurgitation is in my future

Once again, I made it through the night

Sun, 10 Jul 2005

I would say that last night was rough but, really, it was quite exciting to deny my "friend" another glimpse at my nakedness. It would have been easy to accept his invitation of a threesome at our swingers club; the opportunity to quench my thirst for random sex where I am in complete control, but I declined. My refusal last night was akin to the sight of every hard dick in the room watching me writhe in ecstasy while hands and tongues explored every inch of my body, begging for permission to enter, yet being denied at whim. That kind of power was sitting at the back of my throat, morphing into something even more mighty and strong, when all at once and with only the slightest pause, that power released itself from me in the form of a word. "No."

It was magical hearing the word escape my lips, knowing that the power I sought was there waiting all along.

Okay, I could have just said, "John called and invited me to the swinger's club with him and his female friend and I said no." But to be honest with you, I'm horny as fuck right now and just had to let it out. My boyfriend has been out of town for over a week and I'm full-on horny. I've respected our commitment to each other and my promise to myself. Yes, it's been a little difficult, but I made it through. My guy comes back tonight so everything will be cool in short order.

I'm just proud of myself for not giving in when I certainly would have a month ago. I have a new resolve (yeah, I know you've heard that before) and feel so blessed with the strength God has given me. I guess it was there the whole time, I just didn't take advantage of it.

Do I miss my time at the club? Hell yes! I do sometimes miss the power I had in that environment. I miss the randomness of it all. I miss the sex and the sweat and turning men into jelly just because I can. But, it's not the solution to my problems. The solution really has been my ability to keep the promises I made to myself. It's hard sometimes, but I believe everything in life that's worth attaining is also worth a little struggle along the way.

Finding my voice.... again!

Sat, 06 Aug 2005

There's something to be said for taking responsibility for your own actions, or inactions, as it were. You see, choosing to do nothing is still making a choice. Choosing not to speak when you really should is still making a choice. They're not good choices, but choices nonetheless. It seems as if I've lost my voice, staggering back to my ways of old, in a drunken fit of stupidity and worthless feelings. Why, you ask? Hell, I have no idea. Luckily, however, it's only taken less than 24 hours to figure it out. Back in the day it would have taken months to finally get the courage to speak. Today, I'm like "fuck it!" I've spent a great deal of time trying to fix my emotional self. Today, I'm ready to take on the responsibility for my "inaction" in this situation. I'm ready to be alone if it means again finding my voice. I've just gotten used to the sound and I'm not willing to lose it, even if it means losing the man I love.

Fuck you
Sun, 30 Oct 2005
I've decided that I'm going to be
as crazy as I fucking want to be
and fuck anyone who objects.
Not literally of course.
I'm a recovering sex addict.

The meaning of life...
Sun, 18 Dec 2005
Has anyone really figured out the meaning of life? I'm asking a serious question. Anyone? Anyone?

I sit here at my desk, 12-14 hours a day, and basically have no life. I don't go out. I don't have friends over. My ass has become part of the chair. Thank God I don't work naked or I might have to have the chair surgically removed!

I wonder if I've replaced my sexual addiction with a work addiction? Hm... I think maybe. See, I'm not sure what to do with myself if I'm not working. I'm afraid I may go back to my devious ways. Or not. Hell, I just know that "bored" is not a good thing for me.

Maybe, too, I'm hiding from myself and the personal work I have yet to do...

People tell me that I'm afraid to commit, but I think I'm just not willing to "settle" with whatever or whoever comes my way. Status quo is not my thing. In a relationship, I want the man of dreams to recognize that I am the woman of his. We have to be willing to share the good, the bad, and the ugly. I want to know that he finds me as sexy and intelligent as I find him. I want to know that if I faced some catastrophic event, he'd be there with a shoulder for me to cry on. Fuck. What I really want is someone who's a real human being - someone with real emotions who's not afraid to show them; someone willing to stick it out in the realistic, day-to-day shit that comes up in any relationship. No more runners!!

I really need to get real about the sexual abuse issue. I haven't been working on getting the negative crap out of my head and it's wearing on me a bit. Rewiring all the old feelings and thoughts is very difficult and I haven't quite figured out a good way to do it. Anyone? Anyone?

I need to relearn the word "NO" and use it more often.

That's just the short list of things I need to work on. Maybe I'll make an honest list of things to be worked on, worked out, and taken care of then set some new goals.

"Can I talk to you as a friend?"

Sun, 22 Jan 2006

--- "Of course, we *are* friends."

"Yeah, but we used to fuck and I don't want that fact getting in the way."

--- "Of Course. What's going on?"

"Well, I'm really struggling with my sexual addiction lately and I just don't know what to do."

--- "How are you struggling?"

"I've been horny for days. I can't stop thinking about sex and I joined one of those 'adult' sites where you can find other people with the same demons as you."

--- "Well, there's nothing wrong with that. Have you met any of these people?"

"Yes. Just one, but I have plans to meet three others next week. What the fuck is wrong with me? I know that I'm potentially putting myself in dangerous situations, but I just feel as if I don't have any control."

--- "You could say 'no.'"

"Right. When have you ever known me to say no to sex? Remember, we used to fuck."

--- "Right, but you still have the power to say no whenever you want to."

"That's the hard part for me. I just crave the 'connection' so much. I crave the attention, and the feeling that someone wants me, and the rush of the danger I'm putting myself in. It's like playing russian roulette everytime I meet one of these guys."

--- "You're right and I do worry about that for you. You know I can hold your hand through this, right? I'll be there whenever you need me."

"I appreciate that so much. I mean it's great that you'll be there, but you can't be there all the time. I need to learn to control this shit on my own. Fuck, I know what I should do, but it's just so hard."

--- "What do you think you should do?"

"Instead of holding your hand, I should hold the hand of God. I need to reconnect with Him. I need to lean on Him for the strength I need. What sucks though is that the pull of the addiction is so strong and my mind is so fucked up about it, that it's hard to take hold of His hand and just say 'ok, guide me.'"

--- "I understand that but, Kelly, if that's what you believe will make things better, just have the faith that you can do it. You're a strong woman and you don't have to be defined by your addiction. Re-label yourself and let God take the reins in your life."

"I know dammit, it's just so fucking hard. I have to get my head on straight with what I'm doing. All I've ever known is sex. That's how I connect to people. I know it's the wrong way to do it, but I just haven't discovered what else I'm good for."

--- "That's a bunch of crap and you know it. Kelly, you've come so far in your life, after facing years of abuse, rape, divorce, death, etc. You are a strong woman and you can do it. Yeah, you're afraid, but you've faced much harder and worse situations. What makes you think you can't win this?"

"Maybe that's all I think I have. Maybe I think I'm only good for sex. That no one will want me for anything else. I'm afraid of what I'll be if I'm not a sex addict."

--- "Just take the 'sex addict' label out it for a minute and let's see what we have. You're a great mom, you run your own, very successful business, you're a great friend, a great daughter, and you have talent coming out of your ass if you'd just take a minute and use it. You are a lot of other things that don't have anything to do with sex."

"It's nice to hear. I guess I just need to start believing it myself."

--- "Yes you do. No offense, but quit acting like a fucking victim and get your shit together. You're better than this but you're letting fear guide everything right now. You're letting the fucking asshole who molested you rule your life. You are better than that. Fuck, you piss me off sometimes."

"Ha ha. I know. You're right. Fuck I hate feeling weak and vulnerable."

--- "Vulnerable? What do you think you are every time you go to meet some stranger you've met online? That's vulnerable and just plain stupid."

"Fuck you. I mean that in the most agreeable way possible, you know? Seriously, thank you for putting me in my place."

--- "You're welcome. And fuck you, right back."

Who I Am

Tue, 07 Mar 2006

Who I am is my own damned business
I won't apologize for things I've done
or decisions I've made
My path has nothing to do with
YOUR egotistical or insecure bullshit
That's you, not me

So here's a new set of rules baby...
If you can't handle it
then go away
If you can't deal with the truth
then go away
If you're not willing to look at your own life shit
then don't darken my doorway another minute

I gave you freedom to be yourself
It's your choice to use it
But that mask you wear is getting pretty tattered
and old

You are who you are
Don't apologize for the things you've done
or the decisions you've made
Your path has nothing to do with
MY egotistical or insecure bullshit
That's me, not you

What's our responsibility, you ask?
Learn baby!
Learn from the things we've done
and the decisions we've made
You ever think life brought us together
To learn from each other?

But let's be clear
I am who I am
and I won't wear the mask you hold for me
I won't be something I'm not
And I can't change my past

Deal with me
Or move on

I`m over it
Tue, 21 Mar 2006
My horny phase has passed. Sorry boys. It's just that I saw so
many delicious men this weekend and I wanted some. But, I'm at
a new place in my life now, which means, "no more meaningless
sex." Yes, I still get horny as hell, but I just have to fight the urge
to fuck almost anyone with a dick.

But, thanks to those of you who sent me offers... much
appreciated.

The day I became a survivor

Mon, 6 Jun 2006

Each year, organizations across the country recognize "Take Back the Night," a march and open mike rally to help those who have been victimized by sexual abuse, domestic abuse, and the like, by giving them a voice. I attended my first march while in therapy. I remember watching all the men, women, and children there and feeling as if I weren't in my own body. I couldn't believe that so many people actually cared about the subject and would give of their evening to help someone else.

During the open mike portion of the event, I vacillated between listening to others speak and actually speaking, myself. I chose the latter. I wanted to get up there and name my abuser. I wanted everyone to know how much pain I was in. I wanted someone to care. I got up to the mike and looked out over the crowd of 600 or so and what came out of my mouth was pure anger. I rambled, named my abuser, and got off the stage. About a year later, I moved out of state and stopped my therapy.

Ten years later, I returned to the state because my mother-in-law was dying and needed care. I had been in town for about four months when I heard about the next Take Back the Night Rally. I'm not sure why, but I decided to go again. This time, though, I didn't have that glazed-over look on my face. I stood tall and really saw the pain on the faces of the people there. I was surprised when I looked around and saw one of my co-workers there, as well. We both looked at each other and smiled in that knowing way, talked about nonsense for a few minutes, then marched through the streets with everyone else.

After the march, I stood in line to speak, this time without hesitation. As I listened to the people before me, I recognized myself in them. I could hear their suffering. I could see them grasping for something to hold onto; anything that would help them make it through another day of memories, drug addiction, alcoholism, prostitution, physical abuse, and self-abuse.

When it came my turn to speak, I stood quietly for a moment. I hadn't prepared a speech; I wanted to speak from the heart. I told them that ten years prior was the last time I spoke publicly about my abuse. In the ten years since, I had learned a lot. I'd learned how to set boundaries for myself, I'd learned to love myself, and most importantly, I'd learned the word "no." I told the crowd that I never thought I'd make it to this point; never thought I could, but I had faith. I said, "Wrap yourselves up with the love that surrounds you, believe in yourself, and know, deep down, that you can make it through all the pain you're feeling right now. Have faith. Someday you'll find the word 'survivor' in your vocabulary and you'll wonder when it happened, but you'll be happy it finally did. Your life will change, I promise you that."

I got off the stage and went to stand next to my friend. She looked at me and said, "thank you." I asked her why she was thanking me, and she said, "I've never told anyone this before, but I was raped on my sixteenth birthday. I never told anyone, not even my mom. You've given me the courage to finally tell." For over an hour, we talked and cried and held onto each other. It was then I knew I was indeed a survivor and no longer a victim.

Chapter Eight:
My Walk in Faith

Through the years, I've studied many different religions, along with New Age and Native American teachings, all in search of a place to call home. Until the age of seven, my family attended Catholic Church then we moved to a new city and just quite going. When I was old enough to question what I had been taught, I discovered that I didn't agree with many of the teaching and went searching for something else to believe in. After years of researching various mainstream religions, attending services, conferences, and energy healing groups I finally found my way back to God and now regularly attend a bible-based church.

People often ask how I can believe in God, even after I was abused. They wonder why God would "allow it happen" when He is supposed to love everyone, especially innocent children. I believe in God because I've never blamed Him for what happened to me. My biological father did those things to me, not God. People are given free will and will too often use that free will to do harm. Bad things happen to good people all the time; it's the fault of the perpetrator, not the victim, and not God. There's nothing fair or right about it, I know, but those are the choices they made and we, unfortunately, have to live with them.

Luckily, I've always had the mindset to take strength from what happened to me, instead of letting it defeat me. When I met my friend, Cliff, he saw that strength in me, but knew I was still trying to figure out how to use it.

Cliff is a self-professed street minister who uses his own life experiences to preach the word of God. I was a little taken aback when we first met, mostly because he's very passionate about the Bible, and just as vocal, but I was hungry to hear what he had to say. He told me that if I truly wanted to get rid of the pain of the abuse, I simply had to ask God to take it from me. For three days we argued about it and I finally realized that I had tried everything else I knew to try, so what the hell. That night I prayed about it and asked God to take away my pain. I woke the next morning with a sense of peace and calm I had never known before. It was truly amazing.

I realized that throughout my life I've been a much stronger person than I've ever given myself credit for; all by the grace of God. I've often said that God had my back during all the pain of the abuse, the struggle with my addiction, and now in my recovery, and I know He did. I know that I wouldn't have been able to make it to where I am now without His love, and without Him stepping in when I really needed it.

I still sometimes struggle, but as I continue to study the Bible and pray, the better each day becomes. I'm not perfect, but know that I am blessed, I am loved by the Lord, and I am finally free.

A letter to my Father

Sat, 25 Dec 2004

I love you Father. I know I don't say it enough and that I only come to you when things are rough. I'm sorry for that.

You've lifted me up and carried me when the weight of my burdens was too much to bear. You've helped me to see the good in people when I only wanted to turn away. When the mirror betrayed me, you helped me see beyond it and into your eyes.

I've heard your whisper in a song and in the wind, filling my heart with calm. Thank you, Father, for your love and your Son.

Authors Note: What started out as a letter to my father, very quickly turned into a letter to God. It was Christmas day, and as soon as my fingers hit the keys, I realized that I will never have the father I always dreamed about, but God has always been with me. It was quite an amazing feeling to release some of the "what ifs" I had been carrying around for years.

My confession

Wed, 05 Oct 2005

What I confess today is that my strength appears gone. Maybe it's just hidden away because I'm so tired of all that is me. I'm tired of being so fucking depressed, tired of feeling insane all the time, tired of knowing that I am, and tired of trying to hide it from the people around me. I'm tired of being strong. Today, I would have killed myself if not for my children. I love them too much to put them through that. I know what suicide does to a person and I would never do that to my babies. It's not that I really want to die, but I just want this crap to stop. It just hurts so much.

I keep trying to deal with myself and my problems and just when I think I've got some sort of handle on it, one little thing will throw me over the edge. It's that edge I've been tip-toeing on for quite some time now. I think what it really is, is that I feel like I'm "pretending" so much - like I'm just not being myself. Fuck, I'm not even sure what that is, really. I just know that I'm not me.

I went to the lake today and watched the ducks gliding through the water and thought how nice it must be to be a duck. No real worries, just paddling along in the cool water, eating when the mood strikes and thinking about nothing in particular.

What I really wanted to do was curl up in ball in the middle of the desert and just let nature take me. Instead, I had a talk with God. I don't know if He heard me, but I talked anyway. It's funny. I was driving along wanting to talk to a friend, knowing that I have no one, when I realized that God is really the only one who gives a fuck anyway. I can't talk to my boyfriend because he thinks psychology is bullshit. I haven't talked to LJ in over a month. I can try to reach her between the hours of 3 and 4, that's if she answers her phone, but most likely she won't. My parents would just freak out and blame themselves. A-man is in another state and just started a new job so I can't call him. G would just want to have phone sex. Mr. Pretty would want a blow job. D has her own problems to deal with, most of which she calls me for, so she'd be of no help. I guess God is truly the only one I have to talk to about this shit; probably the best of the lot anyway.

Maybe it's time to just clean house and get rid of what bothers me. First, I have to dump the boyfriend. Then pick through my so-called friends. Then just be me, all by myself, and fuck everyone else. I'm tired of giving any thought to how they feel, how they are doing, and how they are getting along when they don't really give a fuck about me anyway. Funny how when you're on the verge of killing yourself you realize that you really don't have anyone to turn to. You try to trick yourself into believing that you do, but really, you don't. Isn't life motherfucking great?!

In hiding from myself

Fri, 19 Nov 2004

Do you ever just want to run away and hide? I do all the time. Really what I want is for my stress to go away. I want my stomach ache to stop long enough for me to enjoy a cup of coffee. I want to feel happy without being distracted by the worries of life.

Strength is what it gets back to. I am a strong woman, everyone says so, but I feel like such a "pretender" sometimes. I guess I haven't figured out how to be strong and human at the same time.

I've taken up praying, and a lot of it. I pray several times a day now. I know I should not pray only when things are bad, but it's easy to forget when everything is going great. One of the things I've been praying about is thankfulness. I've been telling God that I'm thankful for what I do have because life could be much worse. I'm asking God to help me through the struggles I'm facing right now, but I'm mindful of the fact that it could be I'm learning an important life lesson and just have to take what I get.

Something to believe in.

Mon, 17 Jan 2005

This weekend I had a conversation with a friend and he asked me a question (which I can't think of now), to which my answer was, "I just need something to believe in." At first it was just an answer to a question then it seemed to take on new life - like the words slapped me in the head, waiting for me to take notice.

"I just need something to believe in."

I thought about those words and how true they really are, not just for me, but for everyone. We all need something to believe in or there's no point in getting out of bed every day. Then, me being the over-analytical person I am, though the rest of the weekend about what I truly believe in. What jump starts my heart? What am I passionate about? What infuriates me? And what can I, or am I, going to do about any of it? If I answer those questions, I may actually find out a little more about myself and be led in a direction that's good for me, God willing.

Forgiveness.

August 2008

I hadn't spoken to my biological father for over ten years. The last time I saw him was while he was in the hospital after suffering a stroke and heart attack. I spent three hours driving to the hospital, praying all the way, and wondering what I'd say when I saw him. I spent the next three days at his bedside hoping he'd live. He was my father, afterall, and did help to give me life. At that moment, it didn't matter what he had done to me before, he was a human being and he was suffering.

Four days later I went back to the hospital to check in on him after he had open heart surgery. When I walked into the room, he took one look at me and said something sexual, so I turned around and left, and vowed never to see or speak to him again.

Ten years later, my sister called to tell me that her dad, my biological father, had cancer and that his prognosis wasn't good. After her call, I spoke with my friend G, who is a very wise and spiritual man. See, I wasn't sure what to do with the information I had received; should I feel sad, angry, happy? I just wasn't sure. G told me that, as a father, he knows that any father in his right mind would never do the things bio-dad did to me, and that bio-dad must have been very sick to do the things he did. He went on to say that when Jesus was nailed to the cross, he could have asked his father to bring his wrath on the men who had put him on that cross, but instead he said, "Forgive them father for they know not what they do." G said, "Kelly, maybe you should ask God to forgive your father because he knew not what he did."

I thought about it all evening and as I laid my head on my pillow, I asked God to forgive my father. I repeated it over and over until I fell asleep. The next morning I woke up without the burden I was carrying the day before.

On Thanksgiving Day in 2008, my biological father died. I didn't learn of his death until two months later when my youngest daughter called and said she'd seen a folder on my sisters online photo album that read, "RIP Daddy. We miss you." I went to the album but barely recognize the man in the photos. I called my sister to confirm and asked why she didn't tell me sooner. She said she needed time to grieve. See, bio-dad has two families; there's me and my twin brother (who was also abused by bio-dad), and there's his other family, which gives us another three sisters and a brother. Because of what bio-dad did to me and my brother, my sister was afraid we would rejoice when we learned he had died. He was her only parent, so we both understood her feelings and would never have hurt her that way. Instead, I let her talk and told her I was sorry.

After we hung up, I sat and thought about my father and all the things I would never be able to say, and all the questions that would forever go unanswered. I know the likelihood of reconciliation was almost zero, but that little girl inside me still wanted a daddy who would love and cherish her, and never do the things he did.

In the end, I was happy that I asked God to forgive him. It may not have helped him rest in peace, but it has allowed me to do just that.

Chapter Nine:
Then and Now

Recently, I was able to spend some time with my youngest sister. The last time I saw her, she was about four years old and cute as pie. She's 30-years-old now and a beautiful woman, a fantastic mother, and a great wife to her husband. She also knew more about our father than anyone and was willing to share what she knew, without reservation, even knowing what he had done.

The man she described was kind and loving and gentle, and not at all the same man I had known. I was a little jealous, of course, but I'm truly happy she had a good life with him.

The next thing she revealed is that he lost all memory of just before and a few months after his stroke and heart attack, including not remembering his own children. When I saw him in the hospital that day, he didn't know who I was. His remark, although despicable, was not intended for me, his daughter, but for the attractive woman who entered his room. This fact alone has gone a long way in helping me continue to heal.

Most importantly, she told me that he confessed to her all the things he had done wrong before and took responsibility for the hurt he caused. He wanted to talk with me and my brother, but was afraid. I wish he would have faced his fear and tried, but I understand how difficult that would have been.

I don't condone what he did, but I now see him as a flawed and sick human being who made some very bad choices in his life, and at least thought about making it right. That is all I needed to know and I can now sincerely say that I forgive him.

About the Author:

Kelly Boykin grew up in Arizona as a twin and, technically, is the youngest member of the family, with three brothers, two awesome step-brothers (both of whom have passed), a mom (the strongest woman on the planet), and a great stepfather, who she calls dad. Her extended family consists of three sisters and one brother, all of whom she'd like to get to know better.

Ms. Boykin is the mother of two grown daughters who are, undoubtedly, the most amazing and funniest people she's ever known. She has unofficially adopted 35 kids who, at some point, needed a cool mom who would tell them when they're awesome, kick their ass when they're being stupid, set some realistic boundaries and, most of all, let them be themselves.

Ms. Boykin started her career in graphic design and found she had a great talent for it. After divorcing her husband of 11 years, she went back to school and studied marketing and communications. Since then, Ms. Boykin has become an entrepreneur, business owner, unpaid therapist to all her friends, and an author.

With her oldest daughter by her side, Ms. Boykin has started a non-profit organization called "Speak Up," whose mission it is to erase the stigma associated with childhood sexual abuse, rape, assault, and domestic violence, by giving survivors a voice. The Speak Up blog is at speakupsurvivor.wordpress.com.